Home-made
For The Home

Independent Television Books Ltd
in association with Tyne Tees Television

The editors wish to thank the contributors who, at extremely short notice, efficiently and with friendly co-operation provided the articles for this book. We would also like to thank producer Lisle Willis for his encouraging help and remarks, and further thank Betsy Whitaker and Mary Bromly who have been closely associated with the programme throughout.

INDEPENDENT TELEVISION BOOKS LTD
247 Tottenham Court Road, London W1P 0AU

First published 1978
First reprint 1978
Second reprint 1980

© Home-made For The Home, Tyne Tees Television, a member of the Trident Television Group, 1978

© Text (each author holds copyright to his/her own article), 1978

Set in Compugraphic Univers Medium 9/10pt

ISBN: 0 900 72766 7

Printed in Great Britain by The Yale Press Ltd,
Delga House, Carmichael Road, Norwood, London SE25

Contents

The majority of the contributors to Home-made For The Home are members of the Northumbrian Craftsmen. Chairman: Mrs D D Chapman, Old Pottery, Milkwell Lane, Corbridge, Northumberland.

Introduction
by Alison Brierly

When the idea that I should present a television programme all about crafts was first suggested to me, my immediate thought was that I wasn't really the sort of person who would be most suitable; my early school dressmaking attempts were a dismal failure, my lilac, eventually my greyish-lilac, cotton skirt was one of only two to be denied an airing at the school open day. A woven canework basket developed an early, permanent and decided list to the left, and pottery ash trays never caught a glimpse of a kiln door, let alone sweated it out on the inside. Thus early in my school career it quickly became apparent to me, and to my teachers, that if I was born for anything it was certainly not for something that required nimble fingers.

However, second thoughts, and a discovery of the aims of the programme and the ideas behind it, which I had now learnt was to be called **Home-made For The Home,** set me thinking that perhaps a presenter as uninitiated into the art of making it for yourself as I undoubtedly was, wouldn't be quite such a bad idea after all . . . if I could succeed in mastering even the simplest of skills, then anybody could! Also, the programmes weren't to be aimed at the fortunate who had the skill and the ingenuity already to make do for themselves, but at those like me who were beginning to think they might like to try! And anybody (the majority of us it seems these days) who has replenished the larder, clothed the baby, and put aside something for the rates and the electricity bill, will know that there is little enough left to spend on the small luxuries of life that can pretty up a home. A colourful cushion here or there, the replacement of a tatty old chair with a new seat in a fabric that actually matches the room, or a new duvet for the spare bedroom can often be produced without spending a fortune.

Then there was Christmas, birthdays, present-giving time. How I'd so often admired those who, in the giving of a gift made carefully at home, showed skill, enterprise, thought and economy. Again, if *I* could have a go, and what's more enjoy the experience, then anybody could.

One of the constant factors around which each programme was constructed, was that nothing used in the programme was to be too elaborate or too expensive. After all, if materials and equipment together cost nearly as much as the finished item would in the shops, then the temptation to go out and buy it would prove, for me anyway, almost overwhelming! Even so, constantly aware as I was throughout the series, that costs were always kept to a minimum, I was staggered to see in the programme on spinning, dyeing and weaving, that scarves, table mats, stoles even shopping bags could be made so effectively without having to open your purse once. The wool came from the hedgerows, fields and fences, the dye from plants; willowherb, cowparsley, lichen, to mention just three; even the loom, which I thought was a must as a buy, was made quite adequately from an old vegetable box! . . . the ingenuity of it all!

Ingenious certainly, were some of the ideas that sprung from the experts who came to demonstrate their particular craft. (Many of the experts coming to their craft, and discovering their talents quite late in life . . . hope for us all?) Who would have dreamed of using an old eiderdown to make a brand new, beautifully snug and warm duvet; and who would have thought of using a vacuum cleaner to transfer feather fillings in such an orderly neat fashion.

A tip here if you already have a duvet and spend precious minutes thrashing around inside the duvet cover every time its time for a clean one. It comes from duvet-making expert, Elizabeth Holder. The whole process is made simple if tapes are sewn on the inside of the cover and to the end of the duvet. Tie the two sets of tapes together and bingo! covering a duvet is the simplest thing on earth.

In a half hour programme it's just not possible to make instant experts out of us all. Thus the intention of **Home-made For The Home** was to create an immediate interest in us all, show us anything was possible, and encourage us to explore further. Every expert appearing on the programme, almost without exception, emphasised the value of the wide variety of evening classes held now even in the remotest parts of Britain. In these it's possible, it seems, to learn of and become skilled at almost anything; the Women's Institute is another source of encouragement if you wish to make things for yourself, and then there are always more books in the library if you wish for more information.

In order to bring you as many different crafts as we could in the series, each programme dealt with roughly two different but related topics, but the book has a separate chapter for the topics covered. Whether it's making an attractive and highly individual bead choker or bracelet, or producing a batik wall hanging to brighten up a gloomy corner, the processes are explained simply step by step. Important addresses are given, and some detailed information that it was only possible to gloss over during the series.

I will now (smugly I admit in view of my past history) own up to four patchwork cushions in my home, and may even go into partnership with my husband to produce a few simple wooden toys for our little son.

So, whether your intention is to provide your own Christmas presents this year, simply to brighten up your home, or even to earn yourself some pin money, you'll probably need a little effort, some determination, and may I wish you lots of luck.

Alison Brierly, presenter of Home-made For The Home.

Cane seats
by Eileen Elliott

Furnishing, like clothes, moves from one fashion to the next. Currently contemporary interiors are influenced by traditional canework patterns. Carpets, curtain fabrics, upholstery materials and wall coverings all have their canework ranges. This extends through prints and weaves to actual cane panels being used in furniture again.

It would be false, however, to imagine a production line of traditional caneworkers threading and weaving their cane through holes in the furniture frames. In these enlightened times, sheets of cane are imported from native craft weavers, cut to size and wedged into a continuous groove by hammering in a wooden bead.

But our interest is in the restoration of existing chairs in the traditional manner. Speaking of restoration, it was during the Restoration of Charles II that caned chairs found their way into Britain from the much more culturally adorned and fashionable French. Furniture generally became lighter in appearance and canework was used instead of panels on chairs, bedheads, screens etc. Examples of that period are collectors' pieces and even if available, would be beyond the means of most of us.

However, the Nineteenth and early Twentieth Centuries produced great quantities of caned furniture and surprisingly few seemed ever to get mended when broken. The seats, usually the first to go had plywood replacements nailed on top of the ruptured cane and some were upholstered to keep them in service. Few people want these chairs now because not many people can restore them, and even if a restorer is found he is likely to charge a fair amount of money.

Auction rooms and junk shops are the main source of supply for cane chairs that are often in sound condition except for the actual canework. The advantage of such hunting grounds is that the chairs found there can often be bought very cheaply. Remember if a chair has a regular set of holes in the seat frame then it was originally caned. Rarely, if ever, were caned seats left uncovered. 'Squab seats' of about 25mm to 40mm thick were laid on the cane and tied with tapes. In many cases it is obvious to see how the proportions of a chair would fall into place if a 'squab' was added.

So, you have a chair. If it is scratched and needs repolishing, loose in the joints, or covered in layers of paint or polish, strip it, clean it, polish it or glue it *before* you cane it. The exercise of patience — however difficult, pays off at this stage.

The chair is now ready for *you,* now I will tell you how you can be ready for the *chair*!

The cane used for weaving is called rattan, and comes from a climbing plant that grows in eastern tropical regions. The long tendrils of this plant have, under the bark, a hard, shiny layer and it is from this that the cane is produced. The cane of the vine is of a softer, pulpy material, up to 25mm in diameter, and this is also cut into different thicknesses and used for basket weaving.

The cane that we will be using is imported ready-split into six different widths, it comes in hanks of ranging quality, and is sold by weight, at .25kg per hank. (You will need one hank of No 2 cane to adequately cover the seat and back of a small, squarish chair.)

Rattan cane can be bought from the craft suppliers Messrs Dryad Limited, Northgates, Leicester.

Some of the tools you will need may already be in your collection and others can be improvised. A list of tools roughtly in the order you will use them, together with the jobs they will be used for are listed below.

Tools

1 A pair of toenail clippers. These are for cutting and trimming the cane, and would be used initially for cleaning the old canework from the chair.

2 A screwdriver with a shaft slightly smaller than the holes in the chair. Cut off the flattened end of the screwdriver (ie that which fits the screw head) and use the remaining shaft for knocking out the old pegs which held the cane in place.

3 A small panel pin hammer to use in conjunction with the screwdriver, and later to knock in the final new pegs.

4 Golf tees. These are used to wedge the cane in position until the chair is completed.

5 A split cane weaving bodkin. Available from Dryad Limited. This is used for weaving the cane through the two final stages.

6 Although not a tool, you will need some pegs to finally secure the cane in the holes. The easiest method is to buy round dowelling of appropriate size and cut off short lengths to hammer into the holes. Sink the pegs of dowelling to just below the surface with the sawn-off screwdriver, taking care not to damage the cane.

Process

1 First find the centre holes at both the back and front of the chair. Place cane in centre hole at back. Peg it in place with a golf tee. This peg will stay in the chair until completion. Keeping the cane shiny side uppermost, insert it into the front centre hole, and peg it in place. Take the cane under and up through the adjacent hole and peg it, using the peg from the last hole. Return the cane to the back of the chair and repeat the process until you come to the outside edge. At this stage if your chair is not square you will need to weave your cane into a hole in the side frame, which will keep the front to back runs of cane parallel to each other. For clarification see the illustration (Fig 1). Then repeat the process to the other side of the chair.

Fig 1   Stage 1

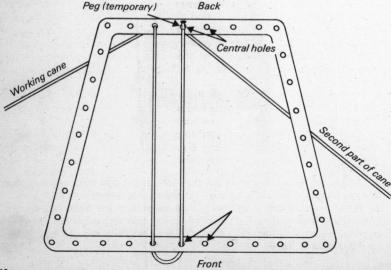

2 The next stage is to take the cane, from left to right of the chair, just the same way as explained in stage 1, only this time there is no need to start in the centre, and the cane is taken over the top of the first layer of cane. On stages 1 and 2 you do not put cane into the corner holes.

3 This is a repetition of stage 1 working the cane over stage 2. As you will now have two canes coming out of the one hole it is important to have them side by side, and not lying on top of one another. Therefore always place the cane on stage 3 to the left of the cane in stage 1.

4 This is a weaving stage, and again you will work as stage 2 from left to right, and starting at the front of the chair. Peg a new piece of cane into the hole nearest the front, but not the corner hole, and then with one hand underneath the chair and one on the top, weave the cane, going over the first vertical cane and under the second. Repeat four or five times and then pull the cane carefully through. Continue doing this in easy stages until you reach the other side. Continue weaving in this manner until you have reached the back of the chair.

At any time during cane work that you come to the end of a piece of cane, peg it with a golf tee and then peg a new piece in the adjacent hole and carry on.

5 This is your first diagonal and you will, at this stage, start to use your bodkin. Going from right to left, start at the back right-hand corner and peg in your new piece of cane. Travelling down, across to the left, take it over the first pair of vertical canes and then straight ahead under the horizontal pair, and repeat. You will then be weaving down towards the left-hand front corner. Take the cane down the nearest hole which will allow it to form a true diagonal. Bring the cane up through the adjacent hole and work back across to the right-hand back corner, in the same way as before. During stage 5 you will find, as the work progresses, that at last you will be putting cane into the corner holes that you have, until now, left empty. On most chairs you will find that, in order to keep your diagonal pattern straight, you will end up with two canes in each of these corner holes. You will find that during weaving you will never miss holes in the back or front of the chair, but at the sides you may have to put two diagonal canes down one hole, or miss a hole completely to keep the pattern straight.

6 This diagonal is worked from the left-hand back corner across to the right-hand front corner. This time you go under the vertical canes and over the horizontal ones. You have now completed all the stages.

7 To finish the seat you will need to peg every hole with your dowelling pegs to secure the cane. Having done this you then take your toenail clippers and trim the ends of the cane away from underneath the chair. Your seat is now ready to sit on.

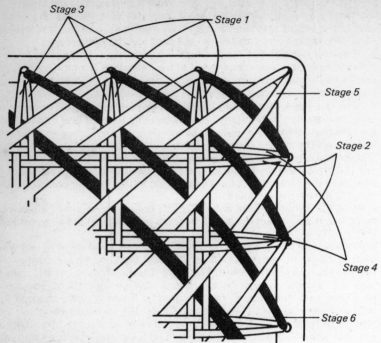

Stage 3

Stage 1

Stage 5

Stage 2

Stage 4

Stage 6

Diagram showing corner diagonals

Useful hints

You will find split cane weaving a much easier and enjoyable process if you follow these few hints.

1   Always use the longest pieces of cane in the hank for your first three stages.

2   Never twist the cane, and always work with the shiny side up.

3   Never allow the cane to become too dry, do not wet it but keep it in a cool room or out in the garage.

4   As in knitting, always work to a firm and regular tension, as the weaving stages progress the cane will become tighter but a reasonable tension must be kept up through the stages, as a sagging seat will look bad and is more susceptable to breaking.

Re-upholstery
by Margaret Carnegie

Modern upholstery, using foam, latex pre-formed shapes, polystyrene, rubber webbing and staples, has completely altered the traditional methods of upholstery. Because new materials have greatly increased the ways and means of attempting upholstery, I will limit myself to describing how to re-upholster a straightforward seat in the traditional manner.

Anyone tackling re-upholstery for the first time, who finds it as enjoyable as I did, should take a trip around the local library or craft shop

Photograph showing underneath of chair and webbing.

for further books on the subject. This is definitely a craft where practical advice from a craftsman is invaluable and to this end upholstery evening classes would be well worthwhile.

You may have an old chair at home with a tattered seat, or even an old chair frame which you would like to restore. Junk shops and auctions are full of slightly damaged chairs, which, with a bit of care and attention, can be re-upholstered and cleaned up to provide a beautiful and practical piece of furniture. Having selected your chair, carefully record all the small details in a notebook. Re-upholstering even a small chair is rarely accomplished in one evening and it is amazing how easy it is to forget the small details. So write down details such as height (or depth) of the chair seat, position of pleats, measurements of the buttons and space between them, position of springs, webbing and tacks, etc.

Materials

Springs (not always necessary)
Hessian (enough to cover the seat area and overlap, twice)
Horsehair or similar fibre
White felt (enough to cover the seat area and overlap, twice)
Calico (enough to cover the seat area and overlap, twice)
Wadding
Top cover (the material obviously depends on your choice and budget. Velvet, leather and cord are all possibles. Those with an eye for detail will want to replace the original cover with material which is as similar as is possible)
Panel pins and tacks
Wood adhesive
Jute webbing ($\frac{5}{8}$" or $\frac{1}{2}$" — calculate length from length of seat, see the diagrams)

The process I will be describing may be modified to produce thicker or thinner seats where desired. Layers of felt or extra horsehair can be added or subtracted to fill or thin the seat.

Preparation

Remove all old material. Start by removing platform canvas (the black lining cloth) from underneath the chair. You can then judge whether or not it is necessary to remove the webbing. If it is sagging at all it really is worthwhile going right back to the frame. Remove the top cover and keep for further reference, go on removing all the various layers of wadding (a fine layer, rather like cotton wool), calico, white or black felt (this looks like compressed Kapok), horsehair, hessian and webbing, making careful notes as you go.

Frames

Now is the time to decide whether the frame of the chair needs attention. Look at the joints, try to move them — if they do move knock them further open with a wooden mallet. Clean out the old glue and use a wood working adhesive to re-glue and clamp together. Clamping may be done by tying thick string or rope round the chair (protecting the legs with pieces of cardboard) then giving an extra tighten by twisting the string with a wooden spoon or large screwdriver.

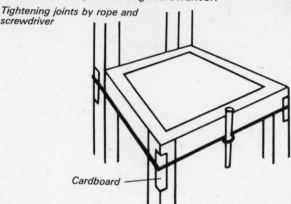

Tightening joints by rope and screwdriver

Cardboard

Any renovating of the wood surface should also be done at this stage. To clean the wood of dirt and old polish use a mixture of raw linseed oil, vinegar and real turps (one part each) and $\frac{1}{4}$ part methylated spirits. Put this mixture into a jar with a screw top lid so that it can be shaken regularly as it tends to separate out very quickly.

Apply the cleaning mixture using a little of the white felt wrapped in a piece of old sheet to make a firm pad. By rubbing the pad (soaked in the cleaning mixture) up and down in the wood the dirt should gradually be removed.

Leave the mixture to dry for about one to two hours before polishing up with a dry duster. Fill in any nail holes with a woodworking adhesive making sure that the adhesive is pushed right into the bottom of each hole.

Webbing

Webbing is a very important process because it is the foundation of all upholstery work. The main object in webbing is to secure the web firmly to the frame and get it very tight. The materials needed are; black and white webbing or jute webbing, $\frac{5}{8}''$ or $\frac{1}{2}''$ improved tacks, (the size depends on the thickness of the frame) and a web-stretcher.

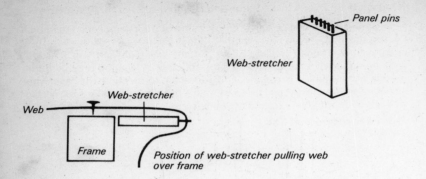

Panel pins

Web-stretcher

Web

Web-stretcher

Frame

Position of web-stretcher pulling web over frame

Use either a proper upholsterer's web-stretcher or make one using a piece of wood 2" x 4" x ¾" and six 1" panel pins. Carefully hammer the panel pins into the narrow end of the wood at an even length. Nip off the heads with a pair of pinchers, leaving six sharp points. This home-made web-stretcher may be used to spike the web and provides a good hand-hold with which to grip and pull the web.

Now you are ready to attach the actual webbing. Start at the back of the seat, having first marked the web positions. For the seat I am describing, six lengths of webbing are used, three down, three across.

Fold the end of the webbing (¾" fold) and tack it in three places, edge, centre, edge. Then tack a further two tacks slightly forward of the centre tack.

First web in position (note pattern of tacks)

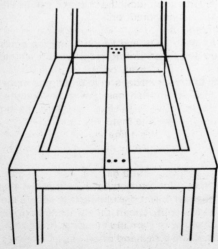

Stretch the web across the frame and tack to the centre front with three tacks, cut off the web leaving $\frac{1}{2}''$ overlap, turn this back on itself and then put in two more tacks. Tack the remaining webs from back to front of the frame. Weave the cross webs through the first webs before attaching to the frame otherwise it will be difficult to get the roll of webbing through the back to front webs. Attach as before.

Weaved pattern of webs

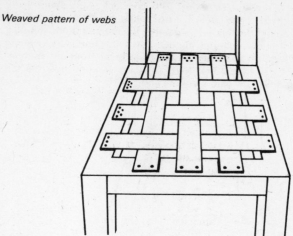

Seat

The hessian base is the next layer to be put on top of the webbing. The materials needed are a piece of 10 oz hessian at least $1\frac{1}{2}''$ larger than the frame and improved $\frac{1}{2}''$ tacks. Tack the hessian onto the frame with temporary tacks (tacks hammered only half-way home so that any mistakes can be put right easily).

To begin, tack the centre back and keep to the straight of the thread and pull tight. Tack centre front turning the raw edge up-over, work out towards the sides working alternatively back to front. Tack the sides in the same way making sure the raw edges are turned up, this will ensure a tighter hessian cover as it is much easier to pull with the fingers and thumbs this way.

Stuffing   For stuffing the seat the materials needed are; stitching twine, (bought at an upholstery shop, it is a fine strong twine with a waxed finish to aid easy stitching) a curved needle about 2-3″ and horsehair or other stuffing such as Algerian grass.

If a chair was originally filled with a ginger fibre that looks very matted and has no 'bounce' you can be sure that this is a coconut fibre and it is best disgarded in favour of, if possible, horsehair. If there was any horsehair in the chair originally, clean this by first steeping in a nappy sterilizing solution. Transfer to an old pillowcase and tie tightly, the horsehair can then be washed by hand or put in the washing machine on the Woollens programme and finished with a fabric softener. This really puts new life into the horsehair. Horsehair mattresses can be bought and gradually washed but be warned, this is a dirty job.

To hold the horsehair stuffing in place it is necessary to bridle-stitch the hessian as in the diagram. Start at the top left hand corner of the hessian, working with a curved needle threaded with stitiching twine, make a 2″ stitch (securing the end with a slip knot). Stitch a back stitch about every $2\frac{1}{2}″$-6″, going straight along the back. Do **not** make the stitch too tight so that it is impossible to get the hair pushed under the stitch but nor should it be so slack that the stitich will not anchor down the horsehair. Having stitched along the back, do one stitch down towards the front of the chair, then work back, parallel to the first row, carry on working towards the front of the seat and finish off with a double knot.

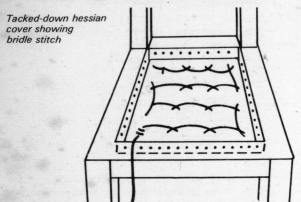

Tacked-down hessian cover showing bridle stitch

Tease out the horsehair, so that it has no matted lumps in it, then, taking a handful of hair, push it under the first bridle stitch so that half the hair is on either side of the stitch. Carry on pushing the hair under all the bridle stitches until the chair is covered. To test whether the hair is covering the seat evenly, stretch out the hands and feel the hair gently with the palms of the hands using a patting motion. Fill in any hollows with a little teased hair — there is no need to try to push it under a bridle stitch.

Felt. Cover the horsehair with white felt. This can be bought at an upholstery shop, and depending on the chair anything up to three layers may be used. When handling the felt never cut it, always tear it apart, this gives it a softer edge and, if using three layers, make sure that each layer is slightly larger than the one underneath. Also make sure that the top layer is not so big that it spreads underneath the tacks holding the calico, which is the next layer to be put in place. The felt is not tacked down — the calico covering will hold it in place.

Calico. The calico must be strong enough to be pulled tight yet fine enough not to be noticeable under the final cover. Use $\frac{1}{2}″$ or $\frac{3}{8}″$ tacks for the calico. Again start from the centre back, fold the calico over double and

18

tack at the centre. Pull the calico forward keeping to the straight of the thread and put a temporary tack in at the centre front. Keeping to the straight of the thread along the back of the chair pull the calico as tight as possible and put a temporary tack at the corners. Having pulled the calico as tight as possible along the whole of the back edge, temporarily tack at 1″ intervals. Pull the calico forward and tension it with one hand while smoothing the top of the seat with the other hand. This helps to set the white felt and horsehair into an even pad underneath the calico.

When tight enough, tack down at 2″ intervals making sure that none of the white felt is caught with the tacks. If the calico can be nipped between the finger and the thumb it is not tight enough. Cut off excess calico to within ½″ turn the raw edge over and tack in between the other tacks. This double thickness of calico ensures that the raw edge is held down.

Final cover. The top cover material needs to be the size of the chair's longest measurement (back to front) plus 4″, and side to side widest measurement plus 4″. (The extra material is needed as a handhold to enable the material to be pulled tight.)

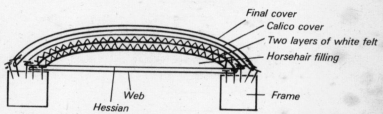

Final cover
Calico cover
Two layers of white felt
Horsehair filling
Web
Hessian
Frame

Do **not** cut the material to shape off the chair. Wait until it is tacked on in place before doing any close cutting. Work with ½″ or ⅜″ tacks, as usual starting at the centre back then to the centre front, and work out from the centre towards the sides putting tacks every 1″. Get the material tight enough so that it cannot be nipped between the finger and the thumb, tack down the sides. Do not turn in the raw edges as this creates a bumpy finish.

Cut away excess material using a sharp bladed knife. A braid can be glued on using a fabric glue but for a more secure edge use gimp pins every 2-3″. These can be bought in various colours to match the fabrics being used.

Finally cut a piece of platform lining (black calico) large enough to cover the underside of the seat. Turn in raw edges and tack to underside of the frame cutting into the corner to fit round the legs.

I hope you have followed through with me this far. Re-upholstery is an extremely satisfying and practical craft which benefits from practice and simple carefulness. It does not have to be expensive, the raw materials are cheap and readily available and the end results are extremely worthwhile.

Duvets
by Elizabeth Holder

In recent years the duvet as been widely accepted in Britain as a useful and convenient bed covering. On the continent, and particularly in Switzerland, splendid duvets have been used for centuries as the traditional form of bed cover. The value of a duvet is the extra warmth it creates compared with an eiderdown and blankets because of the continuous layer of insulation made by the filling.

An eiderdown is stitched through top to bottom and thus has cold spots where the stitching is.

Section of eiderdown

On the other hand a duvet has walls holding the top to the bottom making a continuous layer of air-trapped filling.

Section of duvet

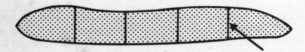

As we all know duvets can be extremely expensive to buy, the best ones reaching several hundreds of pounds. This is mainly because of the expense of the down-filling. Down, which is the fine feathery breast covering found on ducks and geese, can cost as much as £20 per lb. The best quality down is from the eider duck and certain species of geese. Much of the down used in Britain today is imported from China. Considering that 3lb of down is needed for a double duvet, 2lb for a single, then it can be seen that the raw materials are expensive. However don't let that discourage you as there are cheaper mixtures or synthetic materials which may be used to produce a perfectly suitable duvet.

If you can get hold of an old eiderdown — maybe you have inherited one or have managed to pick one up in a jumble sale etc — then the filling in this will be marvellous for a duvet. An eiderdown with good down inside is quite light and will not feel prickly from the feather quills. Terylene can also be used as a filling and I will talk about this shortly.

Size

The duvet can be made any size required. The ideal proportion is 1′6″ wider than the bed or bunk it is to fit, eg a 3′ (91 cm) bed requires a 4′6″ (137 cm) duvet. The length can be made to personal requirements. An average single bed duvet should measure 78″ (200 cm) by 54″ (137 cm) while a double bed duvet should measure 78″ (200 cm) by 72″ (185 cm).

Requirements for an average sized single bed duvet

4 metres of 139 cm (54″-55″) best qualty downproof cambric.
9 metres of 5 cm (2″) wide cotton tape.
2lb of pure down or 'down and feather' mixture or one good quality old eiderdown larger than single bed size.

A single bed eiderdown which has gone thin will not have enough filling for a single bed duvet. A mixture of 'feather and down' will be too heavy, but a mxture of 'down and feather', ie a larger proportion of down, will be suitable.

Method

1 On the glazed side of the cambric mark out in pencil or pen guide lines as in Fig 1.

Fig. 1   The diagram has been distorted for the sake of clarity

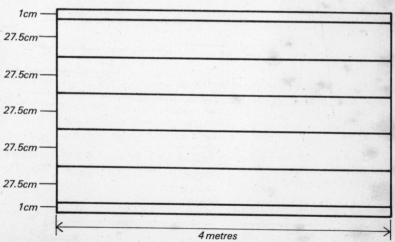

1cm
27.5cm
27.5cm
27.5cm
27.5cm
27.5cm
1cm

4 metres

2 The channels should be as near to 11″ (27.5 cm) wide as possible on all sizes of quilt. This measurement works best.

3 When the lines have been drawn on, fold the cambric in half lengthwise with the lines on the outside and the selvedges together. Make a bag by sewing a double row of stitching down each seam allowance. Do *not* turn this inside out.

Fig 2

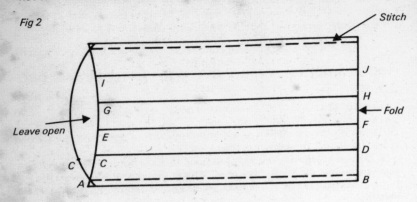

4 Turn in the edge of the bag at AB until it is inside the bag, to the first line CD. Press the two edges formed on the lines CD-CD with an iron as in Fig 3.

Fig 3

5 Cut a piece of the 5 cm wide tape 2.5 cm (1″) longer than the channel line CD. Shape both ends as below. Leave a small seam allowance on the cut part when stitching in.

Fig 4

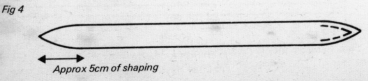

Approx 5cm of shaping

6 Starting at D put one edge of the tape D to the fold D to C and stitch it by machine. Take not more than 2 mm (⅛″) seam allowance. Repeat on the other edge of the tape placed to fold D to C. This forms the wall to the first channel. The process is repeated on each set of lines EF, GH and IJ.

7 When using the line IJ the whole of the bag so far completed will be foded inside the last channel. Take care to sew only the edge of the tape and fold.

8 Do not catch into the stitching any other part of the material. The bag can now be turned right side out by putting the hand inside to the top of the channel and pulling the fabric out.

9 Press with an iron to remove creases.

Filling

There are two methods of filling the duvet. One method can be done by hand by putting approximately 5½-6 oz of down in each channel, if filling a normal length, 27 cm (11″) channel. The filling may be new down, down and feather mixture or taken from an old eiderdown, using a fifth of the eiderdown when filling a 5 channel bag.

Fig 5

Diagram shows approximate fifths of the division of the eiderdown

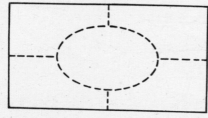

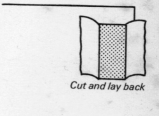

Cut and lay back

A more convenient method of filling the bag is to use a vacuum cleaner as follows. The long tube from the vacuum cleaner tools is first attached to the machine, and the smallest nozzle fitted. The dust bag is next removed and the motor of the cleaner run for a second or two to blow away any loose dust in it.

The opening of one channel of the duvet cover is then tied very firmly to the opening on the vacuum cleaner which would normally take the dust bag. There must be no chance of the cover being blown off or the down escaping.

When using an old eiderdown for the filling, lay out the eiderdown on a firm, flat surface and decide which fifth to use for the first channel (see Fig 5). Cut open a portion of this and lay back the material. If you work with care you will not disturb the down and it can be taken up a *little at a time* by the narrow nozzle of the vacuum cleaner tool. Trying to take up a lot at once will jam the cleaner. It is essential to do a little at a time.

When $5\frac{1}{2}$-6 oz or a fifth of the old eiderdown has been blown into the duvet bag remove the bag and, with the edges of the opening together, fold over $\frac{1}{4}''$ hem, pin and later sew with two rows of fine stitching on a sewing machine, making sure the whole of the opening is closed. Repeat the process for each channel of the duvet bag.

Terylene duvet

Terylene pads of the size required for the quilt and in three different thicknesses can be bought from mail order firms such as Russell Trading Co, 75 Paradise Street, Liverpool. The cover for this should be washable and made from easy-care fabric such as cotton/polyester batiste which is soft and lightweight. Make a bag the size of the pad from this material and with it's wrong side out, lay it on top of the pad, and stitch the seam allowance to the edges of the pad by hand, with large loose stitches. This is to prevent the pad from moving in from the edge of the bag when it is washed.

Fig 6

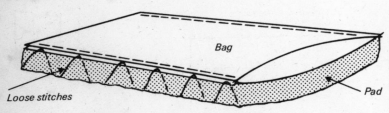

Bag

Loose stitches

Pad

The bag can now be turned right side out to encase the pad. Close the opening and stitch.

With a long thread in a large needle, *loosely* stitch from side to side in a few places to hold the bag in place on the pad.

Fig 7
Do not pull the stitches tight and flatten the pad

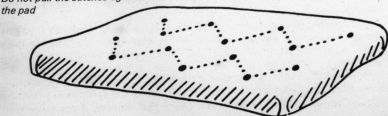

This duvet would be used in a pretty covering bag in the same way as a down duvet. The Terylene duvet is washable and is suitable for use by children or by anyone who is allergic to down and feathers. The down duvet is better not washed but can be dry-cleaned if necessary. It is always improved by an airing out of doors on a sunny day.

I have three duvets of differing strengths that I use for cold and hot weather. However, one thing I never do is to use a sheet with the duvet. This spoils the whole effect of having a duvet which nestles around your body, thus keeping you sealed in. You can make a close fitting cotton cover with little trouble and this should be regarded as your sheet.

Useful addresses

Downproof fabrics may be obtained from most John Lewis stores.
Pure down and feather mixtures may be obtained from:

B Sawtell and Sons Ltd
Down and Feather Purifiers,
Melksham,
Wilts SN12 8BZ

or

Russell Trading Co Ltd
75 Paradise Street
Liverpool L1 3BP

Terylene pads are easy to obtain. Ask you local hardware store or haberdashery shop if you find it difficult to get hold of any of the materials.

Basketry/Canework
by Nellie Renton

Recently watching a series on television describing the attempt by a group of young people to live as an Iron Age community reinforced my belief that a knowledge of weaving was a very basic and necessary skill for the Ancient Britons. Weaving wool for clothing, the weaving of grasses, rushes, twigs and wood for their homes, cooking and storage utensils, and the penning of their domestic animals were all dependent on the basic principles of basketry.

Following the present day fashion for country-cottage-style pine furniture and hand-woven fabrics, the natural look of the modern cane has become very popular, as it blends into any colour scheme. Cane may be used in all forms of basketry to produce countless beautiful and useful items for the home. Elegant bed-heads or intricately woven chairs or tables are beyond the amateur or beginner, so I shall be starting with a simple, but very useful article for the home — a wastepaper basket.

Cane

Centre cane grows in the jungles and swamps of Malaysia and Borneo, being a creeper it can grow from 400-600 feet in length. It is cut and the thorny outer skin removed. The centre of the cane, the pithy part, is then machine-processed to make it smooth and fine, so that it can be used in basket making. You can buy cane from most handicraft shops or direct from suppliers such as Dryads of Leicester. For easy handling it is sold in bundles or hanks in various sizes. For example No 1 is 1¾mm thick, the range continues and includes No 15 at 5mm thick. No 20 is 8mm thick and is used mostly for handles or frames. Prices range from £1.70 to £2.20 per bundle, according to quality. My advice is to use the best cane available for good results with your finished article.

Plastic cane is also widely used. The advantage of this modern product is that, unlike natural centre cane, it does not need damping or soaking to prevent it from cracking. This synthetic cane is ready for use and comes in several colours, which can add interest to the finished article. It is very useful in the making of trays and is slightly cheaper to buy. It comes in size Nos 6 and 8 for staking and No 3 for weaving. I have used this cane, for example, when working on frames for picnic hampers, fishing baskets, work boxes, wastepaper baskets, etc. However, natural cane must be used for any stakes or uprights other than for flat objects such as trays.

Tools

A pair of sidecutters are essential as they enable you to trim any cane ends neatly. A bodkin is also useful, but a steel knitting needle serves the same purpose. Of course, your hands are really your most important tools. It is up to the individual to control the shape and weave of the finished article.

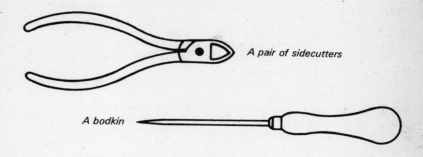

A pair of sidecutters

A bodkin

Bases

I always recommend a beginner to start off by using a plywood, plastic or melamine base and, as confidence is gained with practice, to proceed to the woven base. These bases can again be obtained from handicraft shops or suppliers in round, square or oval shapes of many sizes. They are already drilled for No 6 cane, unless for a special purpose such as log baskets, dog baskets, etc, which will have to be done in heavier cane, for example size 12.

Duo bases

These are very useful and easy to work with and may be bought as a set. The set includes a base (drilled with holes around the edge), a hoop or ring of wood, plastic, etc (also drilled with holes) and stakes that fit the holes, thus matching the ring to the base. The ring is placed on the base with the holes lining up and the stakes are placed in position. The ring will obviously slide up the stakes as is necessary. The weaving is done underneath the ring so that a good shape is easy to maintain. Linen baskets and work baskets are especially suited to these duo bases as the ring serves as a ledge for the lid to rest on. The lid may be either woven or cut from plywood. The actual weave employed is very much the same as the weave used in making a simple wastepaper basket, which I will describe shortly.

Terms used in basketry and illustrations:

Fig 1   Footrac: the border worked underneath a wooden base.
Fig 2   Triple weave or waling: working with three weaves, each going in front of two stakes and behind one.
Fig 3   Triple weaving.
Fig 4   Joining in new weaves when doing triple weave.
Fig 5   Inserting byestakes: an extra stake inserted to the right of the staking to give extra strength.
Fig 6   Randing with one weaver in front of one stake and behind one stake.
Fig 7   Second row of randing.
Fig 8   Joining in new weaver when randing.
Fig 9   Shows how to neaten off joins when finished. All randing joins on the inside of the basket.
Fig 10   Footrac border repeated at top edge to finish off the basket using the double stakes.
Slewing: Weaving as for randing but using two weavers at once.
Slype: A slanting cut on one side of the cane, which is useful when inserting byestakes and handles.

In all weaving the work is chiefly from left to right. The right hand manipulates the weaver and the left hand controls the stakes and hence the shape. Before commencing any work using natural cane, take one strand from the looped end of the bundle, and wind it into neat bundles. Thus it is so much easier to handle and saves tangles and also wastages.

Remember to dampen or soak only as much as you will need. Cane wrapped up damp for a long time will go mouldy. About 5-10 minutes is enough time to soak No 3 cane and the cane can then be used straight from the pail or bowl or wrapped in a towel.

Wastepaper basket

The wastepaper basket will require No 6 natural centre cane. The size will be 10″ across the top with a height of 10″.

1 Cut stakes 18″ long in No 6 cane.

2 Cut byestakes 15″ long in No 6 cane.

3 Commence by soaking the ends of the stakes for 10 minutes only — 3″ to 4″ on one end of the stake to be dampened. (A jam jar is useful for this.) Other than for the footrac, staking must always be kept dry. To work footrac (Fig 1) put dampened stakes through the base so that 3″ to 4″ are showing. Take stake 1 behind stake 2, in front of stake 3 and behind stake 4, leaving about $\frac{1}{4}$″ behind stake 4 on the inside of the weaving. Continue round the base. Thread the last four stakes under the first ones turned down.

Fig 1

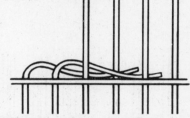

4 The border now being completed, tighten all stakes up to the board, put completed base on a table and press out stakes slightly for easier shaping.

5 Now work four rows *triple weaving* (Figs 2, 3 and 4)

Fig 2

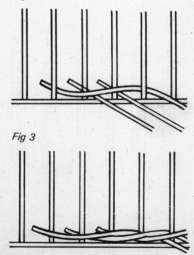

Fig 3

Fig 4

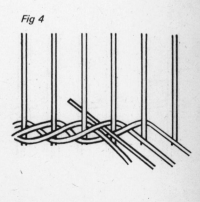

6 Insert *byestakes* (Fig 5)

Fig 5

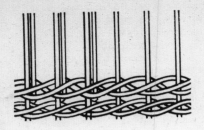

7 *Rand* (Figs 6,7,8 and 9) for 2″ using single weaver. Cut off weaver

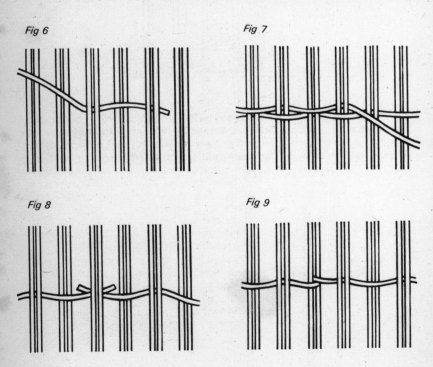

Fig 6

Fig 7

Fig 8

Fig 9

8 Change to *triple weave* for two rows and cut this off.
9 Start at the other side of the basket to give strength and change to *slewing*, which is using two weavers at once, for 3″. Cut off weavers.

10 Do two rows of triple weave and cut off, starting always at the other side of the basket.

11 Rand again for 2″ and finish with four rows of triple weave.

12 Put the basket upside down into a pail of water and soak the stakes down to the last triple weaving.

13 Working with the double stakes, make a *footrac* border (Fig 10), threading the last four stakes into the beginning of the border.

Fig 10

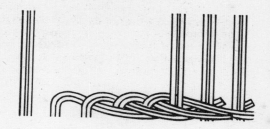

14 Trim inside with sidecutters.

Once a wastepaper basket has been made as a sampler, you can make plant pot holders, roll baskets, work baskets, lampshades and log baskets. To work a lampshade remove the base by soaking the footrac, then reweave the footrac border again and insert a lampshade gimbal or pendant fitting into the basket with raffia. Log baskets are most useful and are easily made using a 15″ or 16″ base of heavy plywood and No 10 or 12 staking and No 6 cane for weaving. Two rope handles complete a log basket, which is really just a heavier and stronger wastepaper basket.

A lovely idea for a bigger piece of cane furniture would be to make up a basket shape, round or square based, using a heavier wood for the base. Buy some ornate wooden legs from the local craftshop and attach them to the base. This could be a beautiful raised log basket or needlework basket, or even a small coffee table, if a basic tray design is used. The possibilities are endless when working in cane, but for now try the wastepaper basket and see how you get along with that.

One final point is that your canework can be protected by a coating of clear varnish. It will keep it clean and give the cane a pleasant shine.

Beadweaving
by Ann E Gill

In this short article on beadweaving I have suggested two items to be made, a choker and a bracelet. The method for producing the choker involves using a beadweaving loom, while the bracelet does not require a loom and can be attempted with the minimum of cost or extra materials. Beadlooms are available in kit form, which comprises a loom, thread, needles and beads. This is suitable for the beginner who does not wish to spend a great deal on a craft before knowing how she or he will like it.

Materials required for the choker

Beadloom   As described above.

Beads   Size 10 (2/0) and size 7 (3/0) Rocaille beads. These are small glass beads from Italy, sometimes called seed beads.

Thread   Buttonhole thread is the most suitable, ordinary sewing thread is too fine.

Beeswax   This is used for waxing the working thread. It helps to prevent tangles and it also helps to strengthen and preserve the thread.

Needles   Size 10 and 9 beading needles. If the holes in the beads are very small it may be necessary to use a size 12 needle. These needles are specially made for beadwork, they are very long and fine with a long narrow eye. Sometimes called Straw needles.

Tape   One inch wide petersham ribbon in several colours (to match beads) is the most useful, however inch wide hem tape may also be used. Bias tape is not successful.

Scissors   A pair of large scissors and a pair of small, sharp embroidery scissors.

Graph paper   This is used for planning the patterns for beadweaving.

Beadweaving; as with conventional weaving; consists of a warp and a weft (lengthways and widthways threads).

Warp threads are held taut on a loom, which in the simplest terms is a frame with grooves through which the threads are placed and held tightly at the opposite end.

The weft thread is that which carries the beads across the work. Unlike conventional weaving this is not a darning movement.

Setting up the loom

The warp Calculate how long the weaving will be. To do this, measure your neck and then double the measurement. This will ensure that there is sufficient thread to attach the warps to the loom and also to finish off the work correctly.

At this point you must also decide how wide the choker is going to be. For instance, a choker which is 9 beads wide requires 10 warp threads plus two extra threads. The extra threads are for the outside warps which are always double warps, this ensures a neater and firmer edge, something like the selvedge on a length of fabric. So, the 9 bead wide choker will have 12 warp threads in all.

Cut 6 threads DOUBLE the calculated length and fold them in half so that there are loops at one end. These threads are attached to the bar of the loom with a half hitch. The threads are then placed through the teeth of the first roller and then through opposing teeth in the second roller, (remember that the outer warps are double and that there should be 9 spaces in the warp). Gather the threads together and hold them over the third roller (this has a single groove), the thin slat of wood provided with the loom is then pushed into the groove in the roller, this holds the threads in place.

The warp threads should have an even, and very tight tension overall.

There will be a lot of thread hanging beyond the grooved roller, this will be needed when you weave; as the warp becomes full you will need to release the threads from the grooved roller, rotate the first roller so that the teeth will not interfere with the weaving, and then wind the work around the bar of wood. Threads are then resecured into the grooved roller.

Planning the design Use the graph paper to plan the design you want to weave. Each square on the paper represents a bead, use either coloured felt tipped pens, or perhaps a symbol, eg X to indicate the colours and their position in the design. It is not necessary to plan the whole of a pattern because when the centre of the work is reached the pattern is reversed.

Process

This is for a 9 bead wide choker, but it is up to the individual to adapt the width. Thread a size 10 beading needle with approximately 1 metre of thread, this is used singly but do not put a knot in the end. Draw the thread through the wax. Have the beads you will be using ready beside the loom. It is easier to pick up the beads if there are a large quantity in a fairly deep container.

1 Sew the working thread to the right hand side outer warps as shown in Fig 1.

Fig 1

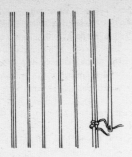

2 Pick up 9 beads and slide them down the thread, pass needle and thread UNDER the warp threads to the left hand side of the loom and take needle in left hand. Pull thread taut so that the beads lie between the warps, and in the 9 spaces.

3 With the index finger of your right hand press the beads up into the spaces in the warp, hold them there.

4 Pass needle and thread through the beads but OVER the warp threads (see Fig 2). Pull thread to tighten.

Fig 2

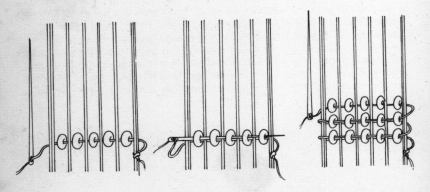

This is the basic weaving process, each row of the weft is made in the same way. To make the pattern you simply pick up the different coloured beads in the sequence indicated by your graph paper pattern.

Attaching a new working thread You will almost certainly need to attach a new thread during the course of weaving. Leave at least 6″ of the old working thread in the needle. Leave this at the right hand side of the work. Thread a new needle with sufficient thread and proceed as follows.

Begin four rows back in the weaving, weave into the rows of beads, drawing the tail of thread into the first of these rows so that it is hidden. When you reach the point where the old thread ran out continue weaving the pattern for about four to five rows using the new thread.

Pick up the old needle and thread, and weave with the thread into the new rows of beads. Pass the needle out through the middle of last row of weaving and to the back of the work. Leave this tail of thread till the work is completed then using small sharp scissors, cut it off very close to the weaving.

Finishing

Remove the work from the loom. Do not cut off the ends of the warp yet. Gather them together and sew through the threads close to the last row of weaving. Make sure you catch all the threads. Do this several times until the threads are secure. Cut the ends of the warp approx $\frac{1}{2}$" from where they are stitched together. Do this at both ends of the work.

Cut enough tape to cover the width of the end of the work, plus enough to make small turnings. Fold the ends of thread onto the back of the work and place the tape, with the turnings underneath over the threads, so that it covers the last few rows of weaving. Hold this in place and using tiny stitches, sew to the side warps, then sew along the bottom of the tape catching the warp threads between the beads to secure. Treat other side and top of tape in the same manner. The other end of the weaving is finished in the same way.

Fasteners Secure a new thread at the end of the work. Bring this out in the middle of the last row of weaving. Pick up enough beads to make a stem, eg 3, you will also require one 6mm wooden bead, pick this up and then pick up three size 10 beads. Pass needle back into the 6mm bead and down the stem (See Fig 3.). Secure the thread in the rows of weaving under the backing tape and trim off.

Fig 3

Main loop of 16 beads

'Bobble' fastener

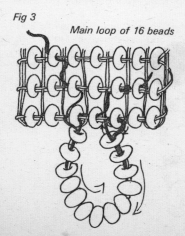

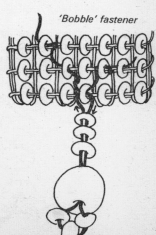

The other end of the work is finished with a loop through which the 'bobble' we have just made, fits. To make this, proceed as follows. Secure a working thread and bring this out next to the 4th bead in the last row of weaving. Pick up 12 size 10 beads and pass needle back into row of beads so that a loop is formed. Take the thread around the loop another time to make sure that it is secure. Fasten off the thread in the rows of weaving under the backing tape as you did with the other end of the work.

NB Diagrams all show different widths of weaving, however the process is the same however wide or narrow the piece of work may be.

Materials for a bracelet using the threading technique

Size 7 (3/0) beads
Size 8mm wooden beads
Buttonhole thread
Size 9 beading needle
Beeswax and scissors

This method of beadwork does not require a loom. The 'flower' shapes are made by taking the needle and thread through some of the beads more than once.

The process

1 Thread a size 9 beading needle with approx two metres of buttonhole thread, this is used double and a knot made at the end. Pull the thread through the wax.

2 Pick up 16 size 7 beads and make a loop by going through the 16 beads a second time. Pull this tight.

3 Hold loop in left hand, pick up three size 7 beads and pass needle and thread down through beads 3,2,1, of main loop, as shown in Fig 4. Pull tight so that the beads are drawn close to the beads of the main large loop and pass needle and thread back up through beads 1,2,3, of pattern (small) loop.

Fig 4

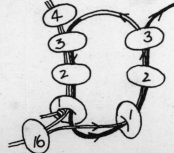

4 Pick up seven size 7 beads plus one 8mm bead and pass needle and thread down through bead 1 as shown in Fig 5. Pull tight and hold firmly.

5 Pick up eight size 7 beads and pass needle and thread up through bead 7 as shown. (Fig 6.) Pull tight and hold.

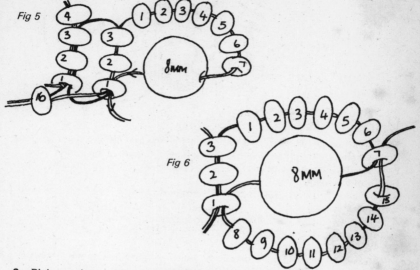

Fig 5

Fig 6

6 Pick up three size 7 beads and pass needle and thread up through beads 14, 15 and 7 as shown (Fig 7.) Pass needle and thread down through beads 16, 17, 18 and pull tight.

Fig 7

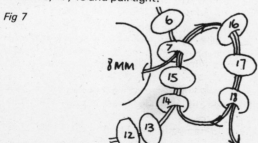

The pattern proceeds as from stage three, until the work will fit around the wrist.

Fastening Make the last complete flower shape plus the three beads you would pick up if you were going on to make another flower. Pick up three more size 7 beads and attach these to the previous three in the same manner. Pick up one 8mm bead and pass needle and thread back into these beads, then back into the 8mm bead. (See Fig 8.) Go around the three beads again and fasten off the thread. The 'bobble' fits into the loop at the start of the bracelet and forms another flower shape.

Fig 8

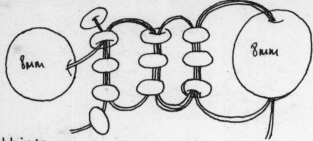

Useful hints

1   Thread used for warp and weft in weaving, and thread used for the bracelet should match as closely as possible the colour of the beads.

2   Tape for the ends of weavings should match, where possible, the colour of the beads.

3   In weaving, never start a new thread by making a knot at the side of the work.

4   When threading up the loom, always use more thread than you really need. This way you will be sure that there is sufficient thread to finish the work.

5   Always have sufficient beads to finish a particular piece of work, quantities less than one ounce are too small.

6   Always wax the working thread.

Useful addresses

Hobby Horse Ltd, 15-17 Langton Street, London SW10
Lots of beads from the above, also beadlooms either in a kit or separately. Threads and needles also available. A comprehensive catalogue is well worth writing for.

Ells and Farrier Ltd, 5 Princes Street, Hanover Square, London W1
Lots of beads, needles and threads available, also beadlooms.

The Needlewoman Shop, 146-148 Regent Street, London W16   BA.
Many kinds of beads also looms and suitable needles and threads.

Fred Aldous Ltd, 37 Lever Street, Manchester.
Beads

All the above offer a good mail order service. Write for catalogues first. Most of these shops also sell books which deal more comprehensively with the craft.

Useful books

Beadwork:The techniques of Stringing, Threading and Weaving by Ann E
Gill. (Batsford)
Beadwork from North American Indian Designs by Marjorie Murphy.
(Batsford)
Creating with Beads by I A Croix. (Little Craft Series, Oak Tree Press)
The Batsford Craft Encyclopaedia by H E Laye Andrews. (Batsford)

An example of Ann's work can be seen on the back cover.

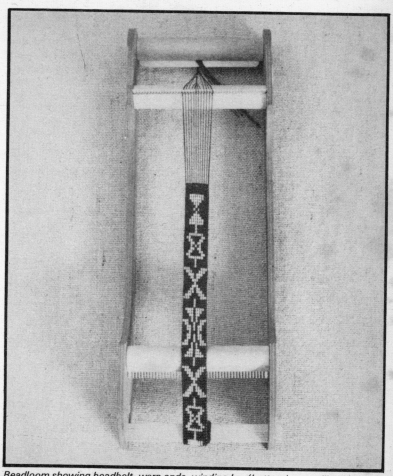

*Beadloom showing beadbelt, warp ends, winding bar (bottom), top rolling bar
and wedge, inside rollers with teeth.*

Embroidery
by Marguerite Collinson

The term 'embroidery' refers to the embellishment or decoration of an existing fabric with stitches and threads. Man has always decorated fabrics in order to personalise them, to give colour and to give them a texture. The first threads that were used were grasses or strips of animal skins, coloured with vegetable dyes worked into slits made in the animal skins with primitive tools. Nowadays we have a huge range of threads available, which have been specifically manufactured for embroidery or have been adapted from some other use and are used because of their interesting texture.

Traditional embroidery was worked by hand, using one type of thread, often in a variety of colours. Modern embroidery uses a variety of thicknesses of threads, which may be worked by hand or machine, and is limited only by the imagination of the worker.

In the programme **Home-made For The Home** Kate Watling demonstrated hand embroidery, showing how traditional stitches may be used on contemporary pieces of work for use in the home.

Placemats

For this embroidery, Kate used the checked gingham and one simple stitch to decorate this useful item.

Cross stitch

Stage 1   Stage 2

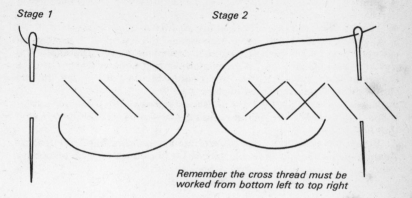

Remember the cross thread must be worked from bottom left to top right

Stages in making the placemats
1 Cut fabric 45cm (18″) by 40cm (16″).
2 Stretch fabric in a round tambour frame.
3 Work embroidery. Leave an end when you start working, which can be finished off later. Any cotton thread can be used for the work — Kate used stranded embroidery thread in a No 8 crewel needle and chose a contrasting colour for her work.
4 Iron on a piece of interfacing 40cm by 35cm to the back of the work.
5 Machine around the edge of the interfacing with three rows of straight stitch embroidery or one row of zig-zag stitch.
6 Fray out the edges.

Cushions

The cushion was inspired by a remnant of curtain fabric. Kate decided to make a cushion with the fabric, but a similar design could be used for a fabric picture, bedspread or roller blind. The fabric was reversed and applied onto a background fabric. This method of work is called *Appliqué*. The tree was applied with couching stitches. *Couching* means to 'lay down'. In embroidery a thick thread is 'couched' onto fabric using a thinner thread, which penetrates the fabric with more ease.

Stages in working the cushion.
1 Cut out background fabric to required size, iron on interfacing to *wrong* side of this fabric.

2   Cut out a second piece of fabric and iron interfacing on to the *right* side of this fabric. From this fabric cut out the tree. The wrong side of the fabric will form the design in this case, as it gives a muted colour and an interesting texture. It is not necessary to use the wrong side, but it can be a good way to use up odd remnants of material.

3   Stretch the background fabric using a picture frame or purchased slate or roller frame.

4   Lay the 'tree' onto the stretched fabric. Tack securely in place.

5   Choose threads for the work. Some need to be thick — these can be several thin threads twisted, knotted, plaited or woven together. The thread for couching could be machine thread, stranded cotton, cotton à broder or linen thread. If the cushion is to be washed, all the threads should be washable and colour fast.

6   It is not usually necessary to finish off the raw edges of your design shape if you use iron-on interfacing, as this fuses the threads in the fabric thus preventing fraying.

7   Couch the thick threads along the branches of the tree. (For greater wearing properties one could machine these free edges prior to decorating them.)

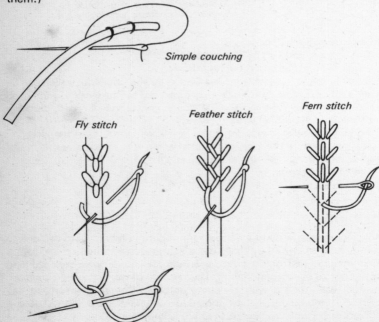

Simple couching

Fly stitch

Feather stitch

Fern stitch

8   Make up the cushion as required, stitching on appropriate fastening in one side. If you make your own cushion pad, make sure it is 3cm larger in width and length than the cover.

42

Creative embroidery using motifs

Although many people enjoy hand embroidery, some do not realise that they can use their sewing machine for creative embroidery.

Owl motif

General instructions   It is best to practice on a spare piece of material before you attempt a complete motif. Below are given the basic instructions which apply to any motif you choose to design.

1   For this type of embroidery, the fabric is stretched in a tambour frame. Place the inner ring of the frame to the right side of the work.

2   Push this inner ring slightly below the outer ring, as this presents a good surface to the bed of the machine.

3   A fine cotton thread is used for all stitchery. A number 30 thread may be used, or, for finer work, a number 50 can be employed. For beginners, a number 50 sewing thread would be preferable.

4   Once you have threaded your machine in the usual way, adjust the machine by removing the presser foot and lowering the feed dog mechanism.

5 Place the frame, with material, under the needle and lower the lever which, in normal use, would lower the presser foot.

6 Lower the needle into the work and bring the lower (spool) thread up to the right side.

7 Hold these two threads as you begin machining. Work a tiny circle to secure the threads, then cut off the two loose threads.

8 Now machine backwards and forwards in a kind of zig-zag until you get used to the machine in its modified state.

9 Try writing someone's name. Remember the line is continuous so PAT is more difficult than Ben or Sue.

10 If you push the work through quickly a large stitch will result. If you push the work through the machine slowly, small stitches will be formed.

11 Next try working in circles.

Owl motif

When you have gained confidence, begin work. For the owl that is shown in the programme, there would be seven different stages. Refer to the complete drawing at the beginning of this article, then make up the owl following the stages illustrated below.

Stage 1

1st colour

2nd colour

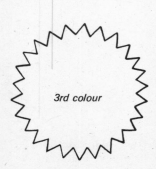
3rd colour

Stage 2

Fill in the eyes and beak in a dark colour.

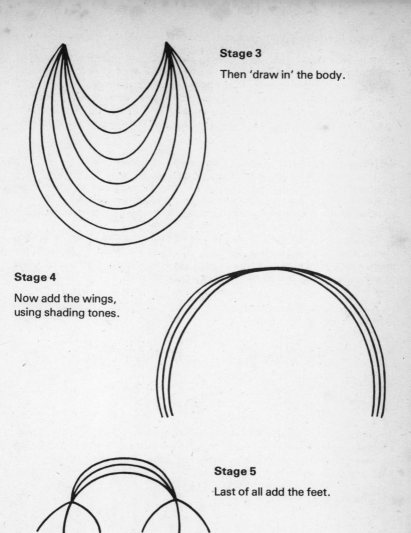

Stage 3

Then 'draw in' the body.

Stage 4

Now add the wings,
using shading tones.

Stage 5

Last of all add the feet.

Note   If you change the top thread colour, the spool thread may be left as before. To prevent this showing on the right side of the work, slightly lower the top thread tension.

The more ambitious worker can now use the free zig-zag stitch, setting the needle on a slight swing stitch. Practice with this stitch — you will find it will fill in areas quickly.

Automatic embroidery

For some lucky people, their sewing machine will produce a range of embroidery stitches automatically. These can be used to decorate a wide binding on a pair of curtains or the edges of a child's garment.

For automatic machine embroidery a special embroidery thread is essential. The material need not be worked in a frame, but the machine must be adjusted. Some fabrics (not transparent) can be stabilized with an iron-on interfacing.

Setting the machine for automatic embroidery stitches
1   Thread the spool with thread and place in spool case.
Increase the lower tension by putting the thread through an additional hole in the spool case, or tightening the tiny screw on the spool case.
2   Thread the top of the machine, ensuring that your machine needle is sharp. *Slightly* lower the thread tension.
3   Commence work by lowering the needle into the work, having set the machine on an appropriate pattern. (There is no need to remove the presser foot.) Try to start at the beginning of a pattern, as it is much easier to match up the pattern at the completion of the work.

Correct and incorrect ways of starting pattern

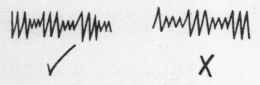

4   Satin stitches produce a firm edge which can serve as an edge finish. For the child's dress, I worked on the pattern line and then trimmed away the seam allowance with a sharp pair of scissors. This is very useful on fine fabrics and curved hems.

Satin stitch edging

Stages in making extension to a curtain

1 Trim off the old hems on your curtain.

2 Cut the binding fabric 2 x final length of required extension to your curtain (plus enough for two seam turnings). The width of the binding should match the width of the curtain, plus a little extra on each edge, which should be turned in and stitched, so that the raw edges are eliminated.

3 Press the binding in half widthways.

4 Pin, tack and then machine one edge of the binding to the curtain, so that the right side of the binding is facing the wrong side of the curtain.

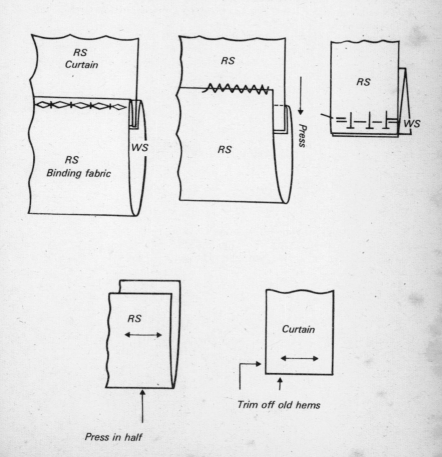

Press in half

Trim off old hems

5 Next turn the binding so that the *wrong side* of the binding now faces the *right side* of the curtain, and either zig-zag the raw edge of binding to curtain,

   or

6 Turn in seam allowance and machine hem down with an automatic stitch.

Useful books

Creative Stitches by Edith John (Pub: Batsford)
Anchor's 100 Embroidery Stitches
Embroidery Stitches by Barbara Snook (Pub: Batsford)
Machine Embroidery: Technique and Design by Jennifer Gray (Pub: Batsford)
Machine Stitches by Anne Butler (Pub: Batsford)

Spinning and weaving
by Naomi Hunt

Weaving has existed in very simple forms from the earliest times. Interlaced structures of thin branches, rushes and reeds were used to make dwellings for shelter, fences to retain the animals and keep out intruders, and baskets for storing and carrying.

Stems, grasses and animal hairs were twisted together to lengthen them, by twisting these under tension a strong continuous thread was made. Hence the drop spindle was invented, which is simply a rotating stick and weight.

Weaving, once it had passed beyond the very simple stages, required a loom on which to stretch out the long verticle threads (*the warp*) through which are woven the horizontal (*weft*) threads. The principle of weaving remained the same though various styles of looms were developed in different parts of the world in response to different needs.

Horizontal weft thread

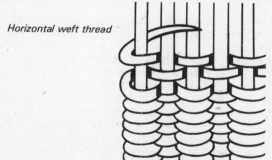

Here are examples of early loom structures, that are still in use today. The *warp weighted loom* has two uprights joined by a bar from which the weighted warps are hung. Looms of this type were used by the Ancient Greeks, and still today by the Chilkat Indians of Alaska who use shredded cedar bark as warp and a large drop spindle to make thread from sheep's wool, dog hair and the fluffy seed head fibre from the rose bay willow herb. Thus the famous Chilkat Blanket is woven.

A *horizontal* or *ground loom* is used by some of East Asiatic nomads. It is set up on the desert floor, simply two bars held in position by stakes and stones. These people live by the seasons and move on when the sheep need new pasture. The loom is simply rolled up and moved on with the trible possessions. In each region the particular dye plants will give a slightly different colour to the wool, so there will be a subtle colour change throughout the same piece of work.

In remote regions of South and Central America the women today use a *back-strap loom.* They set off for the market or a neighbour's house with their loom rolled under their arm. To weave, one end is attached to a fixed point the other to the weaver's waist by a backstrap or belt. Once the loom and its possibilities were understood people could weave long lengths of regularly shaped cloth. In desigining for their functional needs they found opportunity for individual aesthetic expression in the combining of texture, colour and pattern.

Gradually there came an attitude of saving time. How could the weft be speeded through the warp? How could the threads be lifted quicker? Levers and treadles were added to the loom and with the Industrial Revolution came the complete mechanization of spinning and weaving. Thread and fabric could now be mass produced and thus developed the vast textile industry.

As writers on weaving continually point out, each step towards the mechanization of the loom lessens the freedom and creative scope of the weaver. Articles made with care, in the home, for the home have always been greatly valued and handed on from one generation to the next. In times of hardship worn blankets are made into smaller blankets or cushions then finally torn into strips, sorted, dyed, woven and recycled into woollen rugs.

Today is a time of plenty, of mass production, a 'throw away culture' which many people are turning away from in a movement towards self-sufficiency. To weave and spin is not a necessity but a choice. We have the leisure time to make something for the home, or just the right gift for a special person, or see our warped tapestry loom before us as the artist sees a primed canvas. It is the beginning of an artistic adventure.

As the forest and desert people look around their environment for easily available materials and equipment so can we. If we live in the country there is a plentiful supply of twigs and branches for making spindles and looms. Wool for spinning is easily found in the late spring when the sheep get uncomfortably hot before shearing and conveniently rub off their wool on fences and bushes. Later in the year there are often pieces of baler twine to be picked up. If you gather various stems and grasses then dry them out you again have some interesting weaving material, a reminder of a particular visit or holiday.

In the city, markets and back lanes supply an abundance of old bed frames, car roof racks, picture frames and vegetable boxes . . . just waiting to be warped! Railways stations early in the morning yield short lengths of string, with which the newspapers were tied. Excellent material with which to weave a table mat.   Clodagh Alison will probably voice the same warning in her article on vegetable dyes, but as we ask a friend before investigating their wool-box for our needs so it is important to ask before trespassing on other people's property (town or country) in search of weaving materials. An excellent source of cheap wool is the carpet industry which sells 'thrums' or warp ends, often in bags of assorted colours.

There are excellent craft suppliers throughout the country who will send samples and offer mail order services. They stock the traditional spinning and weaving materials and also unusual fibres from different parts of the world, in addition to new experimental yarns.

Remember, what is rubbish to one person is a treasure to someone with their creative eyes open! It has been said 'anything that will bend, will weave'. So there are endless possibilities open to us all.

The more you are involved in a subject the more knowledge you will want to gain, not only by practical experiments but by reading. Public libraries stock many books on spinning and weaving, each year many more splendid volumes are published. Keep adding to your information, but what will be of lasting aesthetic value is what you create with your own hands.

SPINNING

To spin is to draw out fibres and twist them into a continuous thread. The simplest method of doing this is with a drop-spindle.

A Drop-spindle. This is a stick with a notch or hook at the top, there is a weight or whorl fitted on the stick, usually at the base. Whorls have been made of bone, wood, ceramic or stone, sometimes beautifully carved, painted or inlaid. The most rapidly assembled spindle employs a sharp pencil which is pushed into a potato, with a notch cut at the other end of the pencil. Likewise a bar from an old cot can be pushed into a ball of plasticine to make a drop spindle.

There are many methods of spinning; experiment and try out what is comfortable for you. Some spinners walk about, others sit. The spindle may be rolled along the thigh, twirled between the toes or rotated in a small bowl. A lot depends on the plant or animal fibre you are using, remember fine threads, like cotton with short fibres, will need a small delicate spindle and sheep's wool a more weighty structure to pull out the fibres.

Method

1 Sorting: discard any dirty and dried-up bits of wool, make separate piles of the thick and thin fibres, all the time shaking out grass and dust.

2 Teasing: loosen the ends of the wool that might be stuck together with lanolin, lay the prepared wool, the *roving* as it is called, in loose parallel lines. The more care with which this is done will result in a smoother thread. At this stage you can design your wool so that it has subtle colour changes by mixing varying degrees of white grey or brown fleece. Keep the prepared wool in a box if you are not ready to spin, so that it will not get crushed.

3   Spinning: first tie a piece of shop wool to the top of the spindle, that is if you have not yet made any of your own. Holding this in the left hand rotate the spindle clockwise with the right hand, you will feel the fibres tightening against your finger and thumb, now is the time to add the unspun wool. Gradually it will attach itself, keep the fibres lying over the wrist and up the arm out of the way. Keep rotating the spindle with the right hand, and the weight will draw out the fibres into a thread. Continue this way . . . spin, draw out, spin, draw out, adding more wool to the thread in the left hand as needed, organise the fibres into the thickness you require. Keep the spindle rotating and when it reaches the ground wind the thread onto the stick keeping it under tension, attach it with a half hitch to the notch at the top of the spindle. Off you go again, gradually as you relax, the thread, the spindle and your hands all coordinate and you are spinning.

4   Plying: it is possible to use the spindle to ply two pieces of wool together, they are given added strength because they are plied in the opposite direction to which they were spun. Start as before tying the wool ends to the top of the spindle, divide the wool and have an end over each shoulder so that the balls do not tangle, contain each one in a box or pan. Spin in an anti-clockwise direction. Some interesting yarn may be made by plying light and dark shades and experimenting with different thicknesses of wool.

5   Skeining: remove the wool from the spindle keeping it under tension. Wind it around your hand and elbow, remove and lay the skein on a flat surface and tie very loosely in about four places.

6   Scouring: The skein is now soaked in hand-hot water with a little soda for at least an hour or left overnight. Rinse out keeping the water at the same temperature, soak again in soap flakes, gently agitate until the wool is clean, gently squeeze and rinse. Never subject wool to sudden changes in temperature. Hang to dry out-of-doors if possible.

WEAVING

To make a table mat on a vegetable box loom.

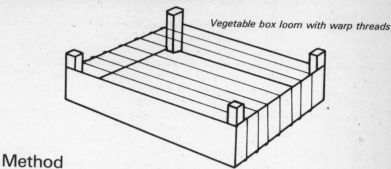

Vegetable box loom with warp threads

Method

1 Warping: use a strong thread wrap it around the box, spacing the threads about ¼″ apart gradually moving across the box, attach both ends firmly with a drawing pin.

2 Weft: the weft is the horizontal thread used for weaving. When making a table mat the threads must be tightly packed down. Organise the colours, ensuring there is enough to repeat the design, check — is this a single (one-off) or a series of mats. Take a piece of wool a convenient length to handle, wind the surplus length into a 'butterfly' and you are ready to weave.

3 Weaving: start weaving on the right of the box, leave a small end to tuck into the back. Pass the weft thread between alternate warps, lifting about four or five at a time on the left hand. Allow the thread to form a wide arc before beating down with the fingers. Continue across the row always arcing the thread as you beat in or your work will become gradually narrower. Turn the thread at the end of the row, being gentle so that there is no pressure on the end warp threads, and begin the next row. With your right hand pick up four or five threads which have previously been woven over, continue to weave across the row. When you need to join, overlap the new thread for about an inch. Pack the threads down so that the warp does not show.

4 Variations: there are many variations which can be made to a plain weave. Beside the weft having colour changes, the warp can also be set up with irregular stripes of different colours, or a regular colour sequence. Different textured wools and threads may be used, and woven at the same time, eg a shiny cotton against a bulky wool.

5 Textured weaves: once you have understood plain weaving, there are methods of changing the woven surface. Here are just a few.

Soumak. Use the same or a contrasting colour. Take the wool over four threads and back under two, and repeat. The combination of threads could also be over two, back over one and repeat. Soumak is set inbetween rows of plain weaving.

Looping. Weave a row, but do not beat down, instead, pick up alternate stitches on a knitting needle, and pull the loops to the required length. Beat down, weave another plain row then another looped row, and pack down tightly to get an all-over pile effect.

Tufting. Rya, Sehna, and Ghiordes are all names of knots, they are all made in a similar way but are different length of tufts. Cut the wool into three inch tufts. Starting on the second pair of warp threads, cover these with the tuft, take the tuft's two ends around to the back and bring them back through the centre to the front, continue to the end of the row. Beat down and weave another plain row. The weaving is continued by a plain, and then a tufted row.

Twining. This is a method used by basket-makers. It is useful to the weaver for separating warp threads at the beginning and end of a piece of work, or adding surface texture. Two weft threads twist backwards and forward between the warps in a continuous figure of eight. Various coloured and textured threads can be used to form a pattern, some colours coming to the front and other floating behind the weaving until needed.

6 Finishing: when the work has reached the required length, cut the wool and weave the remaining end back in. Turn the loom over, cut just a few threads at a time, turn to the front again, take two warps and secure firmly with an overhand knot against the last row of weaving. Continue to tie and cut across the top and bottom of the table mat. Trim the fringe to the length you need, press with a hot iron and a damp cloth.

7 Alternative finishes: the cut warp may be tied again over a piece of doweling for a wall hanging. Alternatively, press to the back and sew under a piece of tape. There are many ways of finishing — find the one that is right for your piece of work.

The whole area of spinning and weaving is a broad and interesting field. What I have attempted to do here, in a limited space, is to encourage you to look around for available materials and try it out for yourself. By using the vegetable box as a starter you can try one or two sample weaves before attempting larger, more ambitious projects. There is a host of excellent reading material on the two subjects, but first try the basics covered here. I'm sure that with the minimum of trouble you could find enough woollen material to spin yourself (dye with Clodagh Alison's vegetable dyes) and weave into a table mat. Once you get this far there will be no stopping you.

One very important point; if you are LEFT HANDED then simply REVERSE all the instructions.

There is a photograph of a beautiful piece of Naomi's work on the cover, the tapestry wall hanging.

Home dyeing with vegetable dyes by Clodagh Alison

Since very early times vegetable dyes have been used by man for dyeing wool and cloth.

The Ancient Britons used woad on their bodies and to dye their clothes and I expect they used many other dyes obtained from plants and minerals as well.

The Roman Legions were clad in cloth, dyed in their various distinctive colours, and I like to think that this is the reason that one of the most useful dye plants 'Lady's Bedstraw' can usually be found beside the old Roman roads and near the sites of Roman settlements.

All the old Scottish tartans were dyed with vegetable dyes and these are still used in Ireland, Scotland, Cumbria and the Hebrides. The well known Harris tweed derives its beautiful soft colours and delicious scent from the lichens with which it is dyed.

The many great sixteenth century tapestries, with their soft, muted tones of colour, which can still be seen in old mansions and museums, were dyed with vegetable dyes. Some of the dyeing methods by that time were quite complicated, and often those who worked in the dye houses had to work in stinking conditions as sometimes urine was used to fix or mordant the dye to the wool, often along with other rather noxious substances!

Many of these dyes have been abandoned as, with the coming of Aneline dyes, dyeing is now simpler, quicker and cheaper. However, there are many beautiful dye colours that can be quite easily produced in the home with plants, shrubs, parts of trees and lichens and a few everyday utensils.

The process is quite time consuming but I think you will find, as I did, that it is a fascinating hobby which takes you into delightful places; onto the moors, by the rivers and streams and many wild places where plants and trees grow.

A word of caution here: never take all the plants from one area; never damage trees or take bark from living trees, it is always possible to find dead bark. Lichens are very slow growing and so only take a little here and there. If you want to gather anything on other peoples' land, houses or fences, always ask permission.

You will need

A large enamel saucepan and/or bucket or stainless steel saucepan and bucket.

One or more wooden spoons or sticks with which to gently prod the wool and move it about.

A pair of rubber gloves.

Good quality soap flakes for washing the wool before dyeing it and a small piece of white soap to test for colour fastness afterwards.

Mordants

These are chemicals which are used to fix the colour to the wool or to lighten, brighten, darken or even completely change the colour obtained. There are many plants which need no mordants and these give substantive dyes. Once you have started I think you will want to go on to obtain a richer and fuller range of colours with the aid of a few simple chemicals.

Alum   This is the most widely used mordant, often mixed with cream of Tartar to bring out the colour. When using Alum the wool may be mordanted with Alum first, using about 3oz Alum, 1oz cream of Tartar for 1lb wool. Put the crystals in sufficient water to cover 1lb wool, warm to dissolve crystals, then enter the previously dampened wool, bring to the boil, turn down heat and simmer for half an hour. Allow to cool. Then remove wool, squeeze out excess liquid and fold in a cloth or cotton bag and store in a cool, dark place for a few days before dyeing this wool. Alum can be obtained from any chemists' shop as can cream of Tartar.

Chrome   (Bichromate of Potash.) This is sensitive to light so you must keep the dye pot covered whilst the wool is being mordanted, and the crystals must be kept in a dark place and out of the reach of children. Wear rubber gloves when handling the crystals as they can irritate the skin.

Tin   (Stannous chloride or crystals of tin.) This gives very bright colours when used. Do not use too much as tin can make the wool harsh. It is best to mordant the wool first with tin before dyeing. Use ½oz of crystals of tin and 2oz cream of Tartar dissolved in sufficient water, to cover 1lb wool. Dissolve the crystals and when the water is warm put in the already dampened wool. Bring to the boil, turn down the heat and simmer very gently for half an hour. Remove from the mordanting solution and rinse the wool. The wool, wrapped in a cloth, should be put away in a dark cupboard for a few days before using it for dyeing.

Iron or copper   (Ferrous sulphate or copper sulphate.) Iron, when added to the dye bath, makes colours darker and sometimes duller. Copper gives green shades. *Either* of these chemicals can be added to the dye bath. After the wool has been simmered for about 30 minutes with the dye plant material, remove the wool, stir in ½oz of iron *or* copper and 2oz cream of Tartar for 1lb wool and return the wool to the dye pot for a further five minute or so.

A good wild flower book is essential to identify the plants you are using and to make sure that you do not use any poisonous plants, which might be dangerous if introduced into the home. Keep a notebook to record both successes and failures and samples of the dyed wool, as this will be very useful to refer to later on. And, of course, most important of all, you will need some wool.

The wool

You can gather your wool from the open heaths and moors or from the hedges and fences of the fields, where sheep are kept, provided that you have first asked permission from the owners of the sheep and fields!

Sometimes, however, the wool from mountain and moorland sheep is very harsh and you might find that, after all your hard work in collecting, spinning and dyeing the wool and then knitting or weaving it, you end up with a beautiful garment which is so scratchy that you cannot wear it!

I would suggest buying a fleece from a sheep farmer, who has sheep of a breed which is known to have soft, lustrous wool. The cost of a fleece will be about £2 to £4, and one fleece should make a large-sized sweater and one or two small garments as well. My favourite fleece comes from the *Jacob Sheep,* and there are many thousands of these sheep in Britain. The wool is beautifully soft and easy to spin and you can get a variety of black, white, brown and grey, all from one sheep, which is quite a bonus when you want good colours! Other nice fleeces come from the *Suffolk Sheep,* the *Border Leicester Sheep,* the *Cheviot Sheep* or the *Teeswater,* to mention just a few of the breeds which you will easily find.

Preparation of the wool

The wool can either be spun first and then dyed in hanks, or it can be dyed before spinning. In either case it must be very thoroughly washed first to remove all the natural oil which normally repels water.

First, soak the wool in cold water for several hours and throw away this water, which will have dissolved away most of the loose dirt. Then wash thoroughly, but gently, as you would a favourite 'woolly', with soap flakes or a good detergent. Rinse well.

Now your wool is ready for use and you can either mordant it in the way I have described or, if you do not wish to mordant it, you can go ahead with dyeing it with your plant or vegetable material.

If you are unable to gather your own wool or obtain a fleece 'straight from the sheep', you can use ordinary pure wool bought from the wool shop, although this is a rather expensive way of doing things. Choose 'natural' rather than very white, bleached wool.

In the next few pages you will see some useful plants which I have used successfully. There are many, many more, but these may be used as a trial to begin with.

Plants to use for dyeing

Sorrel   The roots of common sorrel may be gathered, washed, chopped and put in a muslin bag and boiled until a red colour is produced. Allow to cool, enter the wool, bring the pot to the boil again and then reduce the heat and simmer for about half an hour. Remove the wool from the dye pot and rinse in a bowl of clean water of the same temperature. Test a little bit of your wool to see if the colour stays when washed with soap. If the colour is what you want, rinse wool well and hang out to dry. If not, simmer for a little longer.

Lady's Bedstraw   The roots of Lady's Bedstraw may be treated in the same way to obtain a pretty pinkish colour.

Rosebay or **the Greater Willow Herb,** which grows in great profusion along river banks and on waste sandy ground, can be used to obtain beautiful shades from pale gold to dark old gold. The flowers, stems and leaves can all be used. Put these into the dye pot together with the wool, bring to the boil and then simmer until the required shade is obtained.

Blackberries   Every mother knows what blackberries can do to children's clothes! The berries will give blue to purple with Alum mordant. Young shoots, gathered in the spring, will give black. First boil the shoots and wool for about half an hour and then add a little iron mordant to give you black.

Bilberries give lovely shades from pale lavender to purple or dark blue.

Trees   Of the few trees I have chosen, the leaves of the *Alder* will give shades of pale lemon yellow to old gold and orange, and *Larch* will give green, from the pine needles which it sheds in autumn, and brown, if the bark and fir cones are ground up, soaked for a few days and then used in the same way as the other dye plants. *Oak bark* will give brown, but it should be soaked for some days and then boiled for an hour or two before entering the wool. *Oak galls* or *'oak apples'* as I used to call them, will give black. They must first be broken up and then ground down.

Lichens   There are many varieties of lichens and nearly all give beautiful colours, ranging from a pale pinkish cream to a bright tan and some soft greens. They mostly need no mordants and give useful, very fast colours. If you add a pinch of copper sulphate to *Usnea* you will get green. It can be found hanging from old trees and on rocks. *Parmelia saxatilis* is commonly found growing flat on rocks and old stone or brick buildings. Used on its own, it will give a yellow shade. *Ramalina subfarinacea* is usually found growing on rocky cliffs and walls near the sea. It will give a good, strong shade somewhere between orange and tan.

The list of plants which will give good and interesting colours is almost endless and is far beyond the scope of this book. However, here are the names of a few plants which I have tried successfully, listed with the mordants to use.

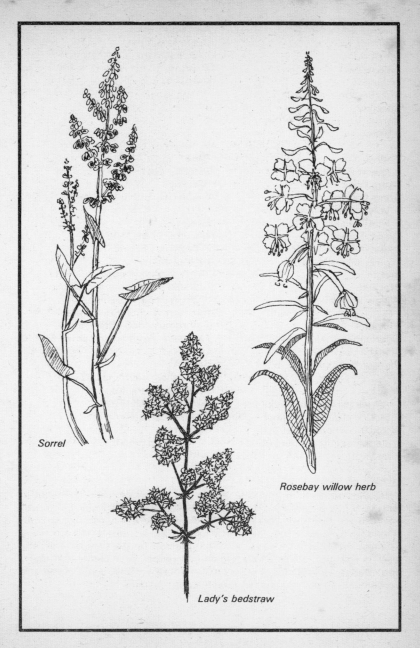

Sorrel

Lady's bedstraw

Rosebay willow herb

Orange and gold
Beetroot + Alum
Onion skins
Alder leaves
Lichens
Snapdragon flowers
Rosebay
Himalayan Balsam + Alum
Wallflowers + Alum

Yellow
Ragwort + Alum
Dyers Weld + Alum
Gorse flowers + Alum
   very bright yellow.
   Use 6″ spikes (stalk
   and flowers), cut
   and boiled whole for
   paler silvery yellow.
Broom
Bracken
Willow leaves

Purple
Elderberries + Alum
Blackberries + Alum
Damson + Alum

Black
Larch leaves + ferrous sulphate
   (added after about ½ hour boiling)
Blackberry shoots + ferrous
   sulphate (added after ½ hour
   boiling)

Red and pink
Begonia + Alum
Lady's Bedstraw + Alum
Meadow Sweet roots + Alum
Raspberry juice + Alum
Strawberries

Blue
Blackberries
Bilberries
Grape Hyacinths

Green
Horsetail or Marestail +
   Alum or Chrome
Willow leaves
Tansy + Alum (copper sulphate
   added after ½ hour and later a
   pinch of ferrous sulphate)
Nettles + Alum (with a pinch of
   chrome added after ½ hour)
Fat Hen + Alum and cream of Tartar

Brown
Pine cones + chrome and iron
Bark from many trees
Birch bark + chrome
   — pinkish brown
Sorrel root
   — pinkish brown

You will probably find that your results are not all the same as mine! In fact, very few people do get the same results, as you will see if you read many of the books on this subject. This is largely because dyeing with vegetable dyes is not an exact science but an art, and there are many variables involved. The colours will be affected by the time of year, the type of soil, the location from which you gather your plants and many other things. However, this makes it even more exciting, so go ahead and experiment — you may find new and beautiful colours.

Useful books

The Observer's Book of Wild Flowers
The Observer's Book of Trees
The Observer's Book of Lichens
Country Bazaar by Andy Pittaway and Bernard Scofield (Fontana/Collins)
A Cottage Berbal by Elizabeth Cullum (David and Charles)
British Sheep Breeds (Wool Marketing Board)
The Use of Vegetable Dyes by V Thurstan (Dryad Press)

Useful addresses

Mordants and some of the rarer plant dyes can be obtained from: Eliza Leadbeater, Rookery Cottage, Dalefords Lane, Whitegate, Northwich, Cheshire, CW8 2BN.

The Jacob Sheep Society
Secretary: Peter Summerfield, 55 High Street, Tring, Hertfordshire, HP23 5AG. Tel: Tring 5919

Tie and dye, batik, transfer printing
by Philip Turney

It is possible to produce examples of these three methods of patterning fabrics in the home without specialized or expensive equipment, and the materials required are easily available from craft shops and departmental stores.

TIE-DYEING

Tie and Dye or tie-dyeing is a resist-dyeing process. It consists of tying or knotting parts of the fabric to prevent the dye penetrating the tied or knotted areas when the fabric is put into the dyebath.

Materials

Dylon Cold Dyes, Multi-purpose or Liquid Dyes
   (depending on the fabric used and the method of dyeing employed)
Dylon Cold Fix or Household Soda
Rubber Gloves
Kitchen Salt
Container, large enough to submerge the article to be dyed, or a washing
   machine if you use the hot water method.
Jug to hold 1 pint ($\frac{1}{2}$ litre)
Thread, (strong thin string, sewing cotton, etc)

Cold water method

Wash and dry the fabric to be dyed. Most new cotton fabrics have some finish or dressing in them, this must be removed so boil it with washing powder. After drying, iron the fabric before tying.

Fabrics   Cotton, linen, silk, or viscose rayon

Bind the fabric   Tie the fabric to get the required pattern, (see diagram) or knot the fabric, (see diagram).

Pull up a point in the fabric and tie a thread tightly near the top. Tie another thread further down. Repeat this process as many times as necessary to cover the fabric. Dye the fabric.

Finished tie-dyed motif

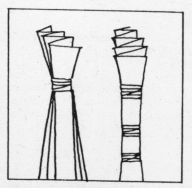

Fold or pleat the fabric, and tie and dye as before

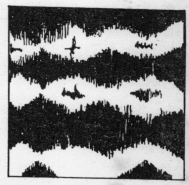

Finished motif

Prepare the dye   Use lighter colour first, and continue through to the darkest for the best results.

ie   Yellow
     Red $\big\rangle$Orange overlap
     Blue $\big\rangle$Purple overlap

Pierce the tin of dye or tins (see instructions supplied with the dyes for the amount of dye required for the article to be dyed). Dissolve contents of each tin in 1 pint ($\frac{1}{2}$ litre) of warm water. Stir well and pour into the container. Add 4 oz (125 gm) salt and 1 packet of *Dylon Cold Fix dissolved in 1 pint ($\frac{1}{2}$ litre) hot water for each tin of dye used.

*1 heaped tablespoon of household soda can be used instead of the Dylon Cold Fix.

Top up with the minimum amount of cold water to cover the fabric.

Dye   Immerse the fabric for 60 minutes stirring occasionally making sure no part of the fabric is left out of the dye. Take out, rinse until the water is clear, remove all or some of the bindings. Wash in hot soapy water, rinse again until the water is clear.

Re-dye   Re-tie or add extra bindings to achieve the pattern required and dye as before. Repeat the binding and dyeing processes as often as necessary to obtain the desired effect.

Hot water method (Using Dylon Multi-purpose or Liquid Dyes

Wash and prepare fabrics as for the cold water method.

Pierce the tin and dissolve powder in 1 pint ($\frac{1}{2}$ litre) of boiling water, stirring well. Add 1 heaped tablespoon of salt for each tin of dye used. Add this dye or ready prepared Liquid Dye solution to the minimum amount of very hot water, to cover the fabric you wish to dye.

Dye   Immerse fabric for 15 - 20 minutes stirring, occasionally, or simmer over heat for 20 minutes. Rinse until water is clear.

Re-dye   Do the same as cold water method.

Tie and Dye is an ideal way of brightening up dull or worn garments, fun for children's clothes, ie T-shirts, blouses, cotton skirts and the bottom of light coloured jeans or trousers. Accessories such as ties, scarves, shawls, handkerchiefs. For the home, tablecloths, tray-cloths, napkins, cushion covers and towels.

Tie and dyed knitting wool.

It is very easy to tie and dye knitting wool. The result is a yarn which has sections of different colours or shades throughout in a random way. The process is the same as for tie-dyeing fabrics. The yarn must be wound into hanks, new or re-wound wool can be used. See that the hank is firmly tied off, then bind tightly round the hank with thread in sections along the length of the hank. (See diagram)

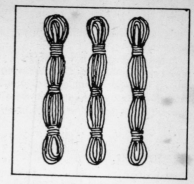

Wind cones or balls into hanks

Wool bound in sections

Dye using the cold or hot water method. After dyeing rinse until the water is clear. Remove bindings if required or add extra ties and re-dye as often as necessary to get the required effect.

Note Two different colour themes produce the best tie and dye effects on knitting wool.

1 Close colours, ie yellows, oranges, browns, or reds, pinks and oranges, blues, greens and turquoise, in fact any range of colours that are close in tone or blend together.

2 Contrasting colours, ie light blue, purple, black, or bright red, yellow, dark blue.

With all methods of tie and dye the only way to see if it works is to try it, in most cases the results obtained by accident are better than pre-conceived ideas.

BATIK

Batik is a method of creating designs on fabric by using wax and cold water dyes.

The waxed parts of the fabric resist the dye, leaving the fabric under the wax the original colour. By applying a second application of wax and re-dyeing the first colour dyed is retained. Continue applying wax and dye until the effect is achieved. As with tie and dye you must dye the lightest colour first, building the design up in stages to the darkest.

Materials

Well washed non-synthetic fabric (cotton, silk, linen)
Batik wax, or a mixture of 75% paraffin-wax and 25% beeswax
Heater to melt wax, as wax is inflammable, the ideal equipment for batik work is an electric hot plate and a heavy saucepan or small double saucepan
Bristle paint brushes
'Tjanting' batik tool, used to apply the wax to the fabric
Wooden frame (old picture frame)
Soft black pencil
Drawing pins
Rubber gloves
Dylon Cold Dyes
Kitchen Salt
Dylon Cold Fix (or Household Soda)
Iron
Absorbent paper (newsprint)

Method

It is important to remember that cold water dyes must be used, as any heat when dyeing will soften the wax and if the water is too hot the wax will come away from the fabric and ruin the batik completely.

The fabric which must be a natural fibre ie cotton, silk, and linen, should be washed to remove any dressing or finish which may be in it. Dry and iron to remove the creases. Then draw the design or picture onto the fabric with a soft black pencil and stretch the fabric tightly over the wooden frame, fixing with drawing pins.

Melt the wax in the double saucepan to the correct temperature, ie when applied to the fabric the wax sinks into the cloth and appears fairly transparent. Keep the wax hot while working. Using a brush or the Tjanting apply the wax to the areas which are to remain white or the natural colour of the fabric.

Prepare the dye   Prepare the cold water dye as instructed in the cold water dye method for tie and dye.

Dye Immerse for 60 minutes and take out, rinse thoroughly in cold water and hang up to drip dry.

Re-waxing and dyeing When the fabric is quite dry replace on the frame and apply wax to the areas which are to remain the colour previously dyed. Allow wax to set, remove from the frame and immerse in the 2nd slightly darker colour. Repeat this process as required to complete the design or picture. (See diagram)

Draw the design onto the fabric.

Stretched and waxed design.

Apply wax to the areas that are to remain yellow. Repeat the dyeing process using a red dye.

Apply wax to the areas that are to remain red, and finally a blue dye.

Removing the wax Place the finished batik between two wads of absorbent paper, and iron with a hot iron, which will melt the wax and allow it to be absorbed into the paper. Repeat until most of the wax has been removed. Wash the fabric in boiling water with a detergent washing powder in it. Rinse off the fabric until the water is clear. Finally iron dry.

Note 1 It is not advisable to pour water containing wax down sinks, allow water to become cold and skim off the solid wax which will be on the surface.

Note 2 It is possible to produce various effects with the wax.

1 After coating a large area with wax, remove from the frame and crumple the fabric in the hands, this will crack the wax, so when dyed it will produce a surface with a crazed appearance, (this is a special characteristic of batik).

2 Paint the wax onto the fabric through pre-cut stencils, cut out of thin card.

3 Shapes, such as circles can be made out of pipe-cleaners, complete with handles, dipped into the hot wax and stamped onto the fabric as often as required.

4 Effects can be obtained by allowing wax to drip from the end of the Tjanting onto the fabric, forming spots, or simply splashed on with a brush.

Batik can be used to make lots of exciting things to wear and for the home: Head squares and scarves, ties. Produce batik on lengths of fabric to make various garments, borders on skirts, wallhangings and pictures, and lampshades (batiks look particularly good when illuminated from behind).

TRANSFER PRINTING

Transfer printing is the simplest of the three methods, it also offers the greatest potential, and will perhaps give the most exciting results. It also needs the least amount of equipment and preparation.

Materials

Fabric — the fabric *must* be synthetic
A packet of 'Finart Fabricrayons' (8 colours)
Iron
Plain cartridge paper
Newspaper

Method

Decide on what you want to decorate. It is advisable to do some test pieces to get the correct setting on the iron (usually set for cotton), and the amount of pressure needed to transfer the design from the paper to the fabric.

Draw out the pattern onto the white cartridge paper, brush off excess crayon specks. The colours change when transferred onto the fabric, the colours become much brighter.

Place the fabric on an ironing pad constructed of several layers of newspaper topped with a sheet of unprinted white paper. Lay the paper design face down on the fabric. Use a clean sheet of plain paper between the iron and paper design. Iron with steady pressure over the entire design until its image becomes slightly visible through the back of the paper design. Make sure the iron does not scorch the fabric. Do not iron excessively or the design may blur, remove paper design carefully.

The decorated fabric can be machine washed using warm water and a gentle action. Do not use bleach, or put fabric in a clothes drier.

Transfer printing is an ideal medium for decorating garments with children's names or initials.

Note If lettering is used it must be drawn out in reverse on the paper to appear the correct way when on the fabric.

Motifs for pockets, borders, in fact anything can be drawn and transferred as long as the fabric is man-made (synthetic). It is advisable to use a fabric which is fairly light in colour. If the pattern is to be transferred onto the front of a shirt or dress for example, a number of sheets of paper must be inserted between the front and back before ironing on the transfer, otherwise the pattern may mark through onto the back of the garment.

For the home, net curtains are excellent for transfer printing. Borders of flowers, or butterflies scattered over the fabric look really good when the curtains are up at a window.

Useful addresses

Most of the materials are available from Art and Craft shops. Dylon dyes are obtainable from most hardware shops and departmental stores.

Information on the various processes can be obtained from:

Fabricrayons	Binney & Smith (Europe) Ltd. Bedford, England,
Tie and Dye, Batik, and Dylon Dyes	Advice Bureau, Dylon International Ltd., Sydenham, London, SE 26.
Books and leaflets on Tie and Dye and Batik, and suppliers of the equipment and materials	Reeves Dryad, Northgates, Leicester, LE1 9BU.

Patchwork
by Dorothy Osler

Patchwork is currently enjoying a great revival of interest. The opportunity to use otherwise wasted scraps of material to make attractive things for the home and for presents, and to exercise one's own individual feeling for colour and pattern, are all combining, with the increase in leisure time, to cause many people to become hooked on a craft which was once a commonplace domestic activity.

First of all, what is patchwork? It is, simply, sewing together scraps of fabric (termed piecing). Usually these scraps of fabric are first cut into geometric shapes before being pieced together. Traditionally, patchwork was most commonly found on patchwork quilts, but a piece of patchwork only becomes a quilt if it is quilted to a lining, with a layer of wadding in between. The term 'patchwork quilt' is often wrongly used to describe a patchwork bedcover which has not been quilted.

The origins of patchwork are lost in history, but it probably began through sheer necessity. Clothes and bed coverings had to last as long as possible, and were patched time and time again to extend their useful lives. Not for our forefathers the attitudes of today's 'throw-away' society. Gradually orderly patterns of geometric shapes emerged, which were passed on from generation to generation in the manner of a traditional craft. The earliest known example of English patchwork is the set of bed furnishings at Levens Hall in Kendel, Cumbria, which was made in 1708. However, it seems likely that patchwork, as a craft, was well established by that time and was practised by genteel ladies to while away the time, and by country women to make use of scraps of fabric and worn clothing to make warm quilts. Indeed making quilts continued as an important domestic craft in country areas through most of the nineteenth century, but, in some areas, the patchwork assumed a lesser importance than the increasingly elaborate quilting. It was left to the well-to-do Victorian ladies to preserve the tradition of patchwork, which they did by producing rather over-elaborate designs in silks and velvets for use in the parlour as well as the bedroom.

Patchwork designs and techniques were also taken across the Atlantic by the early settlers to North America. Here the harsher climate, difficulty in obtaining new textiles and isolation of the new settlers all combined to create an explosion of creativity and originality in the making of patchwork quilts. Throughout the eighteenth and nineteenth centuries patchwork quilts of an amazing variety were produced by these settlers — quilts which were skilfully made, beautifully designed and which showed a sophisticated use of colour and proportion. Anyone whose attempts at patchwork have not progressed beyond the traditional English hexagon would do well to look at some real or illustrated examples of these North American quilts.

How to begin

A good piece of patchwork is a careful combination of colour, design and fabric. It is important to think carefully about these three areas before starting any piece of patchwork.

Colour It is difficult to lay down definite rules about colour, because response to colour is very individual. We usually have strong likes and dislikes about colours. However, when choosing colours for your patchwork consider what colour scheme your finished item has to fit in with and choose your colours accordingly. You should also consider the tone of the colours you use, that is the lightness or darkness of a particular colour. In general, light tones stand out and dark tones recede and this will affect your design accordingly.

Design The patchwork design is the overall combination of shapes which goes into the piece of work. A design can be made up of a single geometric shape, eg the popular hexagon, in which case the design is called a 'one-patch'. Alternatively, a design of one or more geometric shapes can be made up into blocks joined together. This is known as a 'block' design and was the most common way of putting together a patchwork quilt in North America. The American settlers devised an enormous variety of these block designs and gave each of them names. Sometimes the same pattern has different names in different areas. A popular British quilt was the 'medallion' quilt, where a series of patchwork and plain borders surrounded a central pattern called a medallion. Have a look through some patchwork books to see examples of these kinds of designs.

Fabric You can use any kind of fabric in patchwork but, as a general rule, it is *not* wise to try and combine an assortment of different fabrics in one piece of patchwork. They will shrink differently, stretch differently, be of different weights and not perhaps look well together. Cotton is much the easiest fabric to use — it doesn't stretch or fray easily and is available in a wide variety of patterns and colours. Silk and satin and velvets can look nice but are difficult to work. Try not to mix old and new fabrics and wash and press your fabrics before you start.

Once you have decided on your design and colours, it is a useful idea to make a working diagram, to scale, of your chosen design. Graph paper is ideal for this. You can then colour it in to give yourself a visual impression of how your finished work will look. You can experiment with different designs and colours by drawing them out on graph paper in this way.

Templates

Once you have chosen your design and fabrics you are ready to cut out your patches. Your working diagram will tell you how many patches of each fabric you will need (see Fig 1). To cut out the fabric patches you will need a pattern or template for each shape in your design. Patchwork templates can be bought in needlework and craft shops, but it is not difficult to make your own, especially the simple shapes like squares and triangles. However, templates must always be accurate, otherwise your patches will not fit together properly.

If you hand-sew your patches, you will need a paper template for each patch. If, however, you choose to machine sew your patches, the method described below, then you will only need a master template (the size of the patches) from which to draw out each shape on th fabric.

Lay the template down on the fabric and draw round it with a pencil. This pencil line is your sewing line. Cut out the patch, leaving $\frac{3}{8}''$ seam allowance around the pencil line. If you use sandpaper for your template, as I do, and lay it sandpaper side down on the fabric, it grips the fabric as you draw around and gives a more accurate shape.

When you have cut out your patches, you are ready to pin them together and sew them. You will also need to decide in which order to sew them together. If you can, join the patches first into strips and then join the strips together. With block designs you will need to make each block separately, then join them together.

Machine-sewing patchwork

With the limited space available I don't propose to describe how to hand-sew patchwork, since this technique is well known and well described elsewhere. Most patchwork can be as easily sewn on the machine as by hand and machines have been used for patchwork as long as they have been widely available. However, not all designs can be easily machine-sewn — it is best to keep to designs which have straight-line joins and avoid curves and sharp-angled joins.

To pin patches together, take two adjacent patches and, with right sides together, match the pencil lines carefully along the side they will be joined together. Pin at the corners and centre of the line. If you position the pins at right angles to the sewing line, you can machine-sew over them. This way you need not stop the machine to remove the pins. Next, machine-sew a seam exactly along the pencil line on your fabric using a reverse stitch at the beginning and end of the seam. Press carefully. Join all patches together in this manner.

Once the patchwork is complete and carefully pressed it is ready to complete into the chosen article. If you are making a cushion, you will need to put in a zip and lining. A bedspread will need perhaps a border and a lining. Don't spoil your patchwork at this stage by bad finishing — think as carefully about these finishing stages as the patchwork itself.

Machine patchwork (floor cushion)

1 First work out a design for, and decide on the size of, your cushion. To give you a start, reproduced below is the design I used on the programme (Fig 1). You will notice that the pattern is worked in squares, this is the easiest shape to use when making a machine patchwork.

Fig 1 Working diagram of floor cushion — 27" by 27"

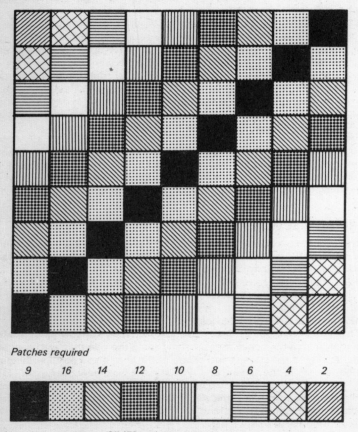

Patches required

| 9 | 16 | 14 | 12 | 10 | 8 | 6 | 4 | 2 |

Each square represents a 3" (76mm) square patch

2 Next make a square template 3" x 3" (approx. 76mm x 76mm) out of medium-grade sandpaper.
3 For a design 27" x 27" you will need squares corresponding to the pattern shown in Fig 1 (81 squares in total).

4 To cut fabric squares, place template on a piece of required fabric and draw round template with a pencil. Remove template and cut out fabric square leaving a seam allowance of $\frac{1}{2}''$ (approx. 12mm) all round.

5 Once you have cut enough squares to complete your design, sort them according to colour or shade for ease of handling.

6 Before machining, lay out all the squares following your design. This checks for accuracy but is also useful for the next step in the process, which is dividing your pattern into strips. The first strip of my design has, from top to bottom, nine squares, each square being made out of a different fabric.

7 To join two squares of fabric pin them together along one $\frac{1}{2}''$ (approx. 12mm) seam line and machine stitch along this seam (see Fig 2).

Fig 2 Pinning together, matching pencil lines and positioning pins at right angles

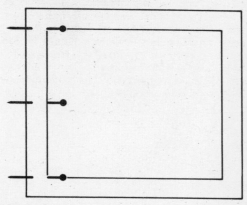

8 Continue joining your squares of fabric until you have formed the first strip of your pattern.

9 Next press the seams. The seams in your first strip should all be pressed to one side, in the same direction. This avoids weakening the seams.

10 The seams of the second pattern strip should all be pressed in the opposite direction from those in the first strip.

11 When all the strips have been completed, and their seams pressed in alternate directions (there are nine strips in our design) sew the strips together lengthwise. These lengthwise seams should be pressed open.

12 Sew lining material on to the patchwork fabric, and then sew on backing material which will form the back of the cushion.

13 Insert zip.

14 Machine stitch remaining sides of cushion. Fill cushion.

NB A good example of Dorothy Osler's work can be seen on the front cover.

Surface and woven crochet by Nina Brissendon

These two methods of crochet, which are simple to learn and do, produce effects that are quite unlike traditional crochet work. Surface crochet can give the look of smocking, tapestry, embroidery or Aran knitting, while woven crochet gives the texture and firmness of fabric in a wide variety of designs.

In this article I have to assume that the reader is aware of the basic techniques of crochet and crochet stitches. I felt that in the space provided it was more valuable to describe the rather unusual crochet stitches I use rather than repeat information that is readily available in other crochet books and articles. Therefore I have limited myself to describing the actual stitches I use. Those of you familiar with crochet will easily apply the stitches to whatever garment or item is envisaged. For the beginner then, a basic crochet pattern book (available from any craftshop) would be a worthwhile aid from the outset.

Surface crochet

Aran crochet, which is one type of surface crochet, has many advantages over Aran knitting, not the least being speed. It is also firmer which means the work does not lose shape, and it gives a wide scope in planning individual garments, as the cables are worked on top after the base pieces have been finished.

Double crochet is the stitch used as a base for cabling, but for a more varied effect other stitches can be used as well, for instance, a sweater could incorporate rib stitch, moss stitch and blackberry stitch, in addition to panels of cabling.

RIB STITCH. The rib is worked sideways so that the depth or welt depends on the number of chains used to start.
Row 1 1 dc into 2nd ch from hook, 1 dc into each ch to end.
Row 2 1 ch (to stand for 1st st), then 1 dc into single horizontal loop which lies just below and slightly to the right of top double loop of next st to last st, 1 dc into turning ch.
  Repeat Row 2 until rib is desired width.
  Change to a larger hook, then work a dc into every row-end down the side of the rib before starting main body pattern.

MOSS STITCH. Worked on an odd number of stitches.
Row 1 (wrong side of work facing) 1 ch, htr into 1st st, * ss into next st, htr into next st, repeat from * to end.
Row 2 1 ch, ss into 1st st, * htr into next st, ss into next st, repeat from * to end.
  Repeat Rows 1 and 2 for pattern.

BLACKBERRY STITCH. Worked on an odd number of stiches.
Row 1 (Wrong side of work facing) (1 ch, yrh, insert hook into 1st st, pull up a loop, yrh, pull through 1 loop on hook only, yrh, insert hook into same stitch, pull up a loop, — 5 loops on hook — yrh, pull through 3 loops, yrh, pull through 2 loops) — a bobble worked, * ss in next st, bobble in next st, repeat from * to end.
Row 2 1 ch, * ss in top of bobble, dc in next st, repeat from * to last st, ss in last bobble.
Row 3 1 ch, ss in 1st st, * bobble in next st, ss in next st, repeat from * to end.
Row 4 1 ch, dc in 1st st, * ss in top of bobble, dc in next st, repeat from * to end.
  Repeat Rows 1 to 4 for pattern.

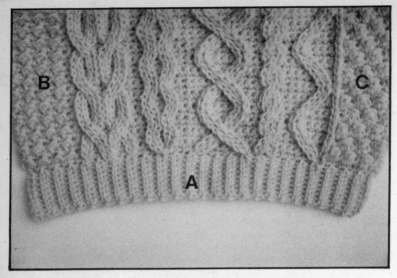

The photograph shows a sample worked in both Aran and Cable stitches. The Aran stitches include: (A) Rib stitch (B) Moss stitch (C) Blackberry stitch. The cable stitches in the central panel are detailed in the following diagram.

CABLING. Worked on a double crochet base with the yarn held behind the base, and the hook at the front.

Make a slip knot (held behind the work) before inserting hook from the front of work in gap between 2 dcs and pull slip knot through to the front, * insert hook back in same gap, pull loop through, insert hook in row above, pull loop through (3 loops on hook), slip last loop through other 2 (dc worked on surface), repeat from *.

Most cables are worked in a double line; that is, when you reach the top of the base material turn the work upside-down, and working to the right of the ridge just completed make another ridge downwards in the same way, inserting the hook in the same gaps between the dcs as before.

Cross the cables alternately over and under.

To cross over a cable make the loops on the hook a little looser, to cover the ridge already made, and continue working.

To cross under, when you reach the crossing point, remove the hook from the loop, slide it horizontally from the unworked side of the cable between the base and the ridge, and pull the loop through. Remove hook again, put it back in the loop the right way and continue working as before.

The size of crochet hook used will depend on the thickness of the yarn, so it is best to do a sample square in the main stitch before commencing a garment. If you find, for example, that using a 6.00 mm. hook with Aran-thickness yarn gives you an easy tension for double crochet and moss stitch, then start a sweater with the rib stitch using a hook two sizes smaller — ie a 5.00 mm. — and use a 5.50 mm. hook for the surface work. If you use double-knitting thickness yarn, then you should use proportionately smaller hooks.

Examples of cable stitches

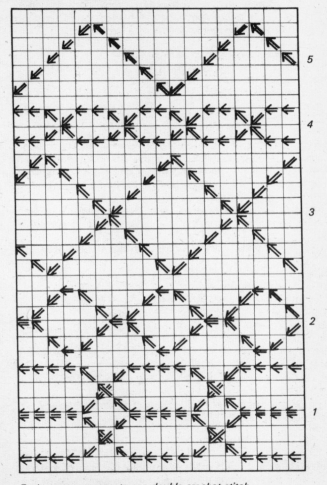

Each square represents one double crochet stitch

1 Lobster claw 2 Honeycombe 3 Diamond 4 Rope 5 Zig-zag

Woven crochet

Woven crochet can give the look of tweeds, plaids, jacquards of quilting, depending on what base stitch is used and how many colours of yarn. In fact, the method used to achieve the fabric is really darning, using an elastic-threader rather than a needle to darn between the stitches of the base already crocheted.

This base can be in double crochet, treble, or pattern stitches such as fan stitch or spaced clusters, but the base stitch most often used for woven crochet is filet mesh, worked as follows:

FILET MESH. Make an even number of chain plus 3.
Row 1   Into the 5th ch from the hook make 1 tr, * 1 ch, miss a ch, 1 tr into next ch, repeat from * to end.
Row 2   3 ch,*1 tr into next tr, 1 ch, repeat from * to last box, miss 1 ch, 1 tr into next ch.
Repeat Row 2 for pattern.

To Weave   Using yarn double, darn elastic-threader vertically through the first line of boxes — that is, over then under alternate chains from bottom to top of base. Stretch the work to relax and even the tension, then turn the work upside-down and darn back in the same line of boxes, alternating the stitches. Stretch the work again.

Many different effects can be achieved using the filet mesh base and this weaving technique in various colour combinations. Here are some examples to try:
1   Use one yarn of mixed texture or colour for both the crochet base and the weaving.
2   Use one colour yarn for the base, and weave in stripes (any number of lines) of one or more contrasting colours.
3   Make the filet mesh in two colours — 2 Rows A, 2 Rows B. Weave with one of the colours only.
4   Make the filet mesh in two colours — 2 Rows A, 2 Rows B. Weave 1 Line A, 1 Line B.
5   Make the filet mesh in two colours — 2 Rows A, 2 Rows B. Weave 2 Lines A, 2 Lines B.
6   Use 3 colours for the filet mesh — 2 Rows A, 2 Rows B, 2 Rows A, 2 Rows C. Weave 2 Lines A, 2 Lines B, 2 Lines A, 2 Lines C.
7   Use 3 colours for the filet mesh — 1 Row A, 1 Row B, 1 Row A, 3 Rows C. Weave 1 Line A, 1 Line B, 1 Line A, 3 Lines C.

When weaving on filet mesh, remember to alternate the lines of darning in the same box; and always begin each line from the same side of the work, so that if you start by inserting the elastic-threader from the back to the front of the work on the first line, do the same on subsequent lines even when changing colours.

The technique of woven crochet gives lots of scope to the individual in choice of yarns, colour combinations and base stitches. It is best, therefore, before beginning any piece of work, to make sample squares in several hook sizes, and then to weave them. You can then check:

1 which is the right size hook to use
2 whether the colours look effective together when woven
3 how much the weaving has altered the original size of the sample (It tends to become shorter and wider with vertical weaving, so take this into account when calculating the size of the finished article.)

It will be apparent that the two types of crochet described are open to a good deal of individual interpretation, so specific instructions about what yarn and hooks to use are not possible.

Experiment with various textures and plies of yarn and, particularly with Aran crochet, use as large a hook as you can, otherwise your work will be stiff and unyielding. With practice you will discover your own most satisfactory way of working and perhaps evolve new methods for yourself.

Abbreviations used:

ch	chain	dc	double crochet
mm	millimetre	htr	half-treble
tr	treble	ss	slip stitch
yrh	yarn round hook	st	stitch

Macramé
by Sheila Hirst

The word 'Macramé' is thought to originate in the Middle East. The Turkish word *Makrama* means a 'fringed kerchief', whilst in Arabic the word *Migramah* means a 'decorated veil'. Both words have similar meanings and are commonly held to be the source of our word macramé.

There are a number of views relating to the growth of the craft as we have come to know it. Some authorities suspect the Crusaders of having introduced the craft into Europe, whilst others point to the fine examples of decorative knotting carried out by sailors, for whom the activity represented a creative extension of workaday skills.

In England the activity is noted as having been enjoyed by Mary, wife of William of Orange, and became a fashionable pursuit at court, Mary being thought to have been responsible for having introduced it from Holland. Certainly macramé was popular in this country throughout the Eighteenth and Nineteenth Centuries and was still practised up until Edwardian times. With the advent of electricity and the mass production of lace, macramé tended to disappear. It is only in recent years that a revival, originating in America, has been responsible for the renewed interest currently being shown in this country.

Whilst I accept the more specific suggestions concerning the origins of the craft, I enjoy the thought of the basic principles being practised by primitive man. The lashing and knotting of vine, grass, and leather occupied a central role in the problem of survival (examples can still be seen in museums housing anthropological collections). It is also interesting to realise, when seen in this light, that the act of knotting has, in all probability, pre-dated the allied skill of weaving.

I trained as a painter. My own interest in macramé arose as a result of finding it virtually impossible to continue painting whilst looking after a house, a husband, and three small children. The uninterrupted time I required for painting was no longer available. In its place was a sense of frustration at the loss of an activity which had previously been very important to me.

It became evident that I needed something to do which would replace painting, and which would fit into a household routine, where spare time is unpredictable and generally short in duration. Equally, I wanted to avoid complex equipment and messy materials, both of which can lead to disastrous consequences when receiving attention from small children!

I have found macramé to be the ideal craft. Equipment is minimal, the materials are not messy and have the added advantage of being cheap to buy. One can work at odd moments or alternatively spend a longer period. The process of knotting is quickly learned (there are two basic knots). The scope and variety of things to be made is virtually inexhaustible.

Materials

To start with all you will need is a piece of soft insulating board, some string, some pins, some glue, and a sharp pair of scissors.

The board should be of manageable size and is used to support the pins which act as anchors for the string (a cushion cover filled with sawdust or sand also works very well).

The string can be simple household string of the kind to be found at any ironmongers.

The pins should preferably be of the glass headed variety.

A tube of glue, such as Bostik, serves to join extra string where further lengths are found to be needed, and most people have a pair of scissors.

It is of course possible to buy materials and equipment at shops and stores specializing in their sale. The only difference in doing this is that it generally costs far more.

Three basic knots

I have already briefly mentioned there are two fundamental knots which form the basis of macramé: the Half Hitch Fig 1, and the Flat Knot or Reef Fig 2, the majority of other knots which can be used are variations of these.

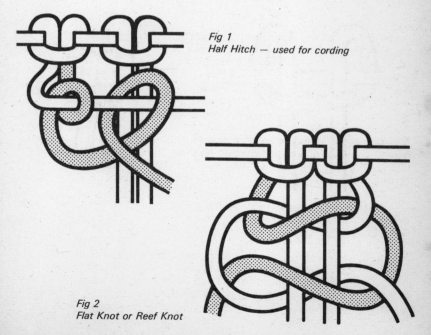

Fig 1
Half Hitch — used for cording

Fig 2
Flat Knot or Reef Knot

It is also necessary to learn how to work the Lark's Head Knot, which is also known as the Reversed Double Half Hitch, and is used to attach the cords to be worked onto a holding cord or, as in the simple belt I will describe later, onto a belt buckle. To work a Lark's Head Knot, cut two lengths of string and double them. Loop each length on to the holding cord as shown in Fig 3.

Fig 3
Lark's Head Knot — used to mount
ends on to holder

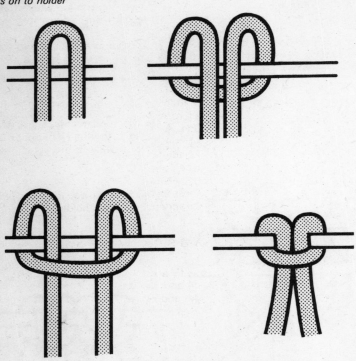

For anyone seriously considering taking up the craft, a book with clear illustrations and diagrams is essential. It should, however, be remembered that the more expensive books are not automatically the best, and that the local library is likely to have suitable books available anyway.

The string

When starting work on an item, the first task is the calculating and cutting the lengths of string to be used. A reasonable expectation is that the piece of string to be worked should be 3 to 4 times as long as the intended item, but as the starting knot ('casting-on' in knitting) generally occurs at the centre of a length, then the string should be cut to lengths which are 6 to 8 times as long as the intended item. The heavier the string, the longer it will need to be. It is, therefore, a good idea to practice knots with the string to be used; this will give you a fair indication of the length needed.

The knobs on the back of an upright chair are a useful support when measuring the lengths of string.

The lengths of string are then attached to a holder. Many different and interesting objects can be used as a holder, obviously the choice will depend upon what is to be made. A length of cord pinned across your 'soft board' for the purposes of making a braid or fringe: a belt-buckle when making a belt: wire lampshade frames and pieces of driftwood are among the many things that can be used.

For a simple but satisfying exercise in macramé, follow these instructions for making a belt. These instructions provide the basic pattern for all sorts of items, including the very popular plant holders.

Materials required for a simple belt

A plain belt buckle

White cotton twin (For a belt with a finished length of 27" or 28" the lengths should be between 14 and 19 feet long. If this length seems unworkable, use half the length and make a join half way through your belt.)

T-shaped pins

A pair of scissors

A tube of glue

Process

1 Measure off four lengths of cotton twine and double them to make eight. Start mounting on to the centre bridge of the buckle using the Lark's Head method (explained earlier). Secure the belt buckle on to insulating board using pins and start knotting using flat knots as described in Stage 2 of this process (see Fig 2).

2 Using the first four lengths on the left, take the cord on the left and the cord on the right, leaving the two centre cords, over which the knot is to be worked, free. Pass the cord on the left over the two centre cords leaving a loop of cord out to the left. Take the cord on the right and pass it under the left cord and under the two centre cords, and up through the loop made in the left cord. To work the second part of the knot, bring the cord which is now on the left under the two centre cords and over the top of the cord which is now on the right, again leaving a loop on the left hand side. Take right cord over the two centre cords and down through the loop on the left hand side. Pull tight. Repeat the process with the other four cords.

3 Starting on the second row using all eight cords, use the four centre cords to make the knot (that is, by following Stage 2 of the process), leaving two cords on either side free (four cords in total). The third row is an exact repeat of the first row and the fourth row an exact repeat of the second.

4 Continue in this way until the belt is the required length.

5 To finish off, take the cord on the left and lay it horizontally across your work. (This cord is called the leader). Now work one row of cording as follows (see Fig 1). Take the next cord on the left, which lies next to the leader, and wrap it up and over the leader cord twice. Take the next cord on the left and repeat. Work three cords in this way until you have reached the centre. Then take the cord on the right and repeat the same process in the opposite direction. Next take the two centre cords, which have been the leaders, and with scissors work them into the back of your work. Cut the ends and secure them with a touch of glue. Secure the rest of the cords in the same manner. The end of the belt should then be a tidy V-shape which can fit quite easily into the buckle.

Useful books

Introducing Macramé by Eirian Short (Batsford)
Far Beyond The Fringe by Eugene Andes (Van Nastrand Reinhold Co.)
Macramé, Creative Design In Knotting by Dona Z. Meilach (George Allen and Unwin Limited)
The Technique Of Macramé by Bonny Schmidt Burleson (Batsford)

Polyester resin
by Yvonne Ellison

Resin is a very versatile and fascinating substance, which has the added attraction of requiring the minimum of equipment to use it successfully. As a craft medium it is, therefore, ideal for use in the home. It can be made into jewelry, paperweights, book-ends, wall plaques, trays, table tops and many other attractive and unique articles to brighten up your home.

Resin is a clear, liquid substance which, when mixed with the correct amount of hardener (supplied with it), sets very hard. Beware, this process cannot be reversed! Because it is a liquid it must be put in a mould to set. The finished article is usually built up of several layers. As it is a clear substance, it is an ideal material to use for embedding any number of things. Fragile articles can then be handled without mishap; small flowers and fossils, for example, when set in a dome-shaped resin mould are magnified and so are seen more easily; collections of feathers, pebbles, stamps, coins and badges all make suitable embedding subjects. However, any plants or flowers, or anything which has moisture in it, must be thoroughly dried before using. This is done either by pressing or hanging the article in a dry atmosphere, or by placing it in a dessicant such as Borax, Alum or Silica Gel for a few days.

Moulds

There are a number of different shapes of moulds sold for use with resin and they are usually made of polythene or porcelain, but one can use many articles found around the home just as effectively. Oven-proof dishes and cups and basins made from thick glass, glazed porcelain or enamel can be used, provided they are well polished with a non-silicone wax polish, and are wider at the open end than at the bottom. This last point is important because when the resin has hardened you would be unable to remove it from your mould if you used a concave or convex shape. Even wood can be used if given a few coats of polyurethane varnish or covered with strips of shiny adhesive tape. Hard plastic dishes and food containers are unsuitable as the resin reacts and dissolves the surface. Margarine tubs are also unsuitable as heat is usually generated in the setting stages and the tub will probably shrink, as anyone who has poured hot water or fat into one will know! It is possible to make moulds using melted latex rubber round a particular shape such as a door knob. Here one *can* make round, convex or concave shapes because the rubber stretches when pulled off. But with this kind of mould the surface finish of the resin is not good and usually needs polishing. Another way to obtain these rounded shapes is to make a square, domed or rectangular shape from the resin which you then file, shape and sand with wet or dry silicon carbide papers. Start with the coarse grade paper then use the medium and lastly the fine. Finally polish well with metal polish.

When embedding in domed- or curved-based moulds, the layers are always done upside down, as the widest part becomes the base of the casting.

Moulds with perpendicular sides and flat bases can be used either upside down or built up from the top. The casting sometimes has to be extracted with a small rubber suction pad, but in all cases immersing the whole thing alternately in very hot water, then upside down in very cold water, will loosen the casting which will eventually fall out. Leave the casting for about ten minutes in each temperature, repeating the process until it loosens. However, as a rule, after a few days the casting will have hardened thoroughly and have shrunk slightly so that it will tip out without you having to employ the above procedure. Because the resin shrinks it usually sets in a slight curve on the final layer and the edges are often sharp and need to be sanded down. Unlike other substances the resin does not set and dry thoroughly in oxygen, so the surface of the final layer will probably remain slightly sticky. If this sticky layer is the *top* of the casting, it needs to be sanded down until it is level, and then polished. If this surface is to be the *base* of the casting, that procedure can be avoided by covering the base with self-adhesive baize or felt. It really is always worth the extra time and patience needed to sand down your article until smooth. Use both the wet and dry papers wet, as this avoids dust. Afterwards polish it with many applications of metal polish to get a perfect surface.

Using colour

As well as using the resin clear, it can be mixed with colour pigments which are made in a wide variety of intermixable colours. These are either translucent or opaque and can be used to give a base opaque layer on table mats, plaques, etc.; to give a tinted, translucent colour to embeddings; or again to produce clear, translucent and opaque layers in a casting of sculpture or in pieces of jewelry.

The resin can also be mixed with other substances — glass fibre for added strength for trays, etc; and dry sawdust or filling powder for a different texture for sculpture castings or chess men.

Embedding

When embedding one must have a layer of set resin in the mould before placing in the article. Once the layer including the article has set, a third layer, about the same thickness as the first, should be added. There are ways of overcoming this rather long process, one of which is to tie a thread of glass fibre to the article, and you can find out more ways from the many books on the subject — there are sure to be some in your library. Also most of the companies making the polyester resins have leaflets about the many ways of using their products and helpful information and advice departments.

Buying the resin

The resin can be bought in several size containers from about 300 grams to 5 kilos. Thin grades of resin are available for small castings and a thicker consistency resin for large, deeper castings. Resin can be bought at DIY, craft and hobby shops and often in the toy departments of large stores. Resin should not be used by children without adult supervision. Someone is needed to make sure they follow all the Do's and Don'ts which are listed below.

Do's and Don'ts

Do wear old clothes and protect the table surface with layers of old newspapers.

Do wear barrier cream or rubber gloves on hands if skin is sensitive — the hardener especially can cause irritation.

Do have some acetone handy for cleaning stickiness from hands.

Do wash thoroughly with water if any splashes get on face or in eyes.

Do make sure the mould is put to set on a level surface.

Do make sure air bubbles are not trapped under embedding articles *before* the resin sets.

Do put the mould to set in room temperature (20°C, 67°F). If the air is too cold the mould will take too long to set; if the air is too warm this might cause the resin to overheat and the casting may burn and crack.

Do use the correct type of measuring mug sold for the purpose. Guessing the quantity of millilitres of resin per drops of hardener will be difficult to gauge, and this must be correct.

Do cover the mould during the setting stages to keep out dust and to confine the fumes and odour which are rather strong. An inverted cardboard box is a good method.

Do read the instructions for each particular make of polyester resin (this is usually enclosed in the pack), especially about the amount of hardener to add if the resin is of the thick grade. The amount of hardener must be cut down in this case, or the heat process may be too severe and cause cracking, or even burning of the embedded article and possibly cracking of the mould.

Do keep the resin in a cool, dark place when not in use, as it has a limited shelf-life and does tend to go thick and lumpy in time.

Don't work in a confined, unventilated room as the odour can be rather overwhelming.

Don't mix resin or leave it to set near food, as the food can be contaminated by the strong fumes and odour.

Don't work near an open fire — the chemicals are flammable.

Don't smoke.

Don't let any moisture enter the resin or mould as this will cause cloudiness.

Don't ever mix the colour pigments in the measuring mug as it could contaminate it for use with clear resin later. It must be mixed in another container.

Nature picture

A nature picture can be made by casting a number of small ice-cube size mouldings, each with a nature inclusion, then making a large mould from glass and wood to cast them all together, and finally making a frame for the 'picture' which has built-in 'glass'.

Equipment

Resin with hardener.

Measuring mug.

Moulds — polythene ice-cube moulds.

Mixing sticks — broken clothes pegs, lolly sticks, etc.

Tweezers — saves hands getting sticky when embedding.

Articles to be embedded — pressed, dried flowers, small shells, pebbles, sea-weed, dead insects, etc.

Colour pigment. ⎫ these will only be needed if
Old cup or similar vessel for mixing ⎬ there is to be an opaque or
colour. ⎭ tinted base to the castings

Sheet of glass, approximate size of top surfaces of all the castings when placed together in a square or rectangular shape.

Pieces of wood, approximately 1" x $\frac{1}{2}$" thick to make sides around glass.

Clear self adhesive tape.

Wax polish (of non-silicone type).

Process

1 Polish the moulds well and make sure all the polish is removed with a soft, non-fluffy cloth.

2 Measure out enough resin to cover the base of each mould to approximately $\frac{1}{4}$" (7mm) and add correct amount of hardener. Mix resin and hardener thoroughly and then pour into the moulds. This is the base layer, so if you wish it to be coloured the measured resin should be poured into the old cup and mixed with colour before pouring into moulds.

3 Cover and leave to set until gel stage. (In the correct temperature this will take about 20 minutes.)

4 Insert the articles to be embedded, right sides uppermost and well pressed down to expel any air bubbles. Cover with another layer of resin and hardener, leaving to set as before. Cover with the final clear layer. If the inclusion is heavy, such as a stone, the second and third layers can be done in one pouring, but the amount of hardener must be reduced.

ice-cube casting

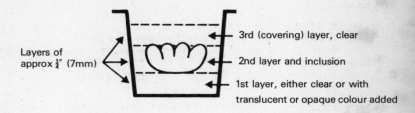

Layers of approx $\frac{1}{4}$" (7mm)

3rd (covering) layer, clear

2nd layer and inclusion

1st layer, either clear or with

translucent or opaque colour added

5 The final layer does not have to be sanded down since it is not exposed to the air, being covered by a further layer of resin. (If the final layer of resin *is* open to the air, you will of course sand it down.)

6 Make the large mould by placing the lengths of wood around each edge of the glass, overlapping the wood at the corners.

7 Stick strips of wide clear adhesive tape to the glass starting about $\frac{1}{2}$" from the edge, pushing them well into the corners made by the wood sides, and overlapping the wood sides by about $\frac{1}{2}$". This must be done as neatly as possible to seal the join between the wood and the glass, as any irregularities will show up on the final casting.

Section of glass and wood mould

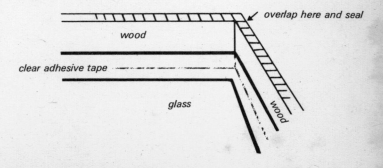

overlap here and seal

wood

clear adhesive tape

glass

wood

8 Polish all the surfaces thoroughly and place the mould on plastic sheeting just in case of leakage.

9 Mix sufficient resin and hardener to cover the mould to a depth of approximately $\frac{1}{4}''$. Insert all the little castings face down into the liquid, making sure no air bubbles are trapped under their surfaces.

10 As it is a fairly large surface leave to dry thoroughly before taking it out of the mould. To make the casting stronger a further layer of resin can be poured into the mould.

11 Sand down any irregularities on the surface of the picture, polish and place in a deep wooden frame to finish the picture.

Useful addresses

Some of the makers of *polyester resins* are:—

Turner Research Limited, Jubilee Terrace, Leeds LS6 2XH

Isopon Inter Chemicals, Duxons Turn, Marylands Avenue, Hemel Hempstead, Herts

Trylon Limited, Thrift Street, Wollaston, Northants NN9 7QJ

There is a photograph on the cover of a beautiful resin tray that Yvonne made.

Candle making
by Jen Darby

Regrettably, candle making is a dying craft. This is sad, because anyone who gives it a try will be pleasantly surprised at how easily, and how cheaply, a colourful assortment of candles can be made.

My very first try was made unintentionally. I had bought a small glass salt pot in a little antique shop, while on holiday. When I brought it home it looked so plain. I was thinking of a way to brighten it up, and thought about filling it up with coloured wax. Not knowing exactly what to do, I melted an ordinary household candle in an old cup. That gave me the wax, but I wanted it coloured. After thinking about what I could use, I decided to grate a small piece of orange-coloured wax crayon into the cup, and waited for it to melt. The result was a beautiful pale peach shade. I poured the coloured wax into the salt pot and, when it was almost set, I put a length of wick, saved from the original candle, in the centre. I was thrilled with the result. The seed was sown!

My next step was to visit the local library. All my knowledge on the subject is from books, and of course, trial and error. By adapting ideas, colour combinations, and seeing other people's ideas, you will easily acquire your own distinctive style. Candle making allows you to experiment with very little waste, as any candle you don't like can easily be melted down and the wax re-used.

Once the interest has been generated you will no doubt want to improve the quality of your candles. This can be done by buying the raw materials which are used to make candles — these are listed below.

Paraffine-wax

As the basis of all my candles I use paraffine-wax. It is easily obtained from craft shops or chemist shops. Different preparations of wax are readily available, and if economy determines the type you buy, I would suggest solid blocks of wax, as these are the cheapest at approximately 80 pence per kilo. Next in line comes flaked paraffine-wax as it is easier to weigh and melt down than the block type. Flaked wax would cost about £1.20 per kilo. You can also buy one kilo boxes of wax, with improving additive already combined with the wax, for about £1.60. As you can see you can make more for your money by using the basic wax and a little extra effort.

I use blocks of wax myself and find them quite satisfactory. Including the small amount of extras you would need, £1 could make you possibly six candles for your home, or six very reasonable gifts for your friends.

Wax additives

These improve the structure of the wax, helping to avoid flaws in the candle and also helping the candle to burn slowly and steadily, without flickering or spluttering.

Sterine (Steric Acid) when added to the wax will make the wax harder, the candle easier to remove from the mould, and will improve the colours, making them more vivid. It will also make white candles a pure, snow white. If you mix Sterine with your wax it also helps the dye disc to melt efficiently, so it's a good idea to add the Sterine and the dye to the wax at the same time. A good guideline for the amount to use is one part Sterine to ten parts wax.

Microcrystalline hardener is an alternative to steric acid as a hardener and is one of my favourite aids as it improves the complete candle structure in one operation. It is available with high and low melting points so that different decorating techniques can be fairly easily obtained.

Beeswax   The use of beeswax in candle making goes far back in history, to Roman times and before. It is very easy to recognise because of the faint sweet smell of honey and the yellowish gold colour. It is obtainable in blocks, but although candles can be made totally from beeswax this would be quite costly. So it is best to use beeswax as a supplement to paraffine-wax (you would also have to add a hardener). A candle with beeswax added is a distinctive milky-white colour and burns more slowly than any other type of candle. Its flame is also softer, as can be seen in church candles. Beeswax is also available in coloured sheets, usually with a honeycombe pattern on the surface. These sheets can be rolled around a length of wick to make very striking candles quickly and simply.

Wax thermomenters

These will give you an accurate reading of the wax temperature at different stages during the melting process. (Do not use a medical thermometer as it will not stand up to the heat.) Wax thermometers are available from craft shops from about £1.50.

It is important to use wax that is not too hot as this could alter the colour of the wax, and also cause bubbles, resulting in tiny holes appearing in the finished candle.

Wicks

The correct thickness of wick is also important when the candle is burning. If the wick used is too fine it will only melt a small diameter of wax in the centre of the candle, although this can be used to gain a special effect — that of seeing the flame glowing through the outer shell of the candle. Below is a general guide to wick size.

Candle Diameter		Wick
1″ — 3″	use	15 ply
3″ — 4″	use	24 ply
4″ plus	use	30 ply

Dye

Wax dye is obtained in concentrated discs. One disc is enough to colour two kilos of wax. Powdered dye is used for very large quantities of wax but I would not advise anyone to use this type of dye unless they had had a lot of experience with wax. It can be very messy and precision is essential.

If you really get stuck children's wax crayons in small quantities, or even small amounts of old lipstick can be used! I must stress though, that crayons and lipstick can leave particles of grit that will fall to the base of your candles.

Discs are also available that will dye, perfume *and* add the wax improving substance at the same time. Thus when the candle burns the chosen perfume will gently scent the room. Just a note here on perfume: it is not possible to use the ordinary perfume that you keep on your dressing table as this has an alcohol base and will not mix with the wax. Non-alcohol based liquid perfume can be obtained from craft shops.

Moulds

Almost anything can be used for a candle mould. Although I do find the simpler the shape, the more stunning the finished candle will look. I use all sorts of things that most of us would normally throw away, for example, toothpaste boxes, yoghurt cartons and paper cups. Small pudding basins, cups, egg cups, ice cube trays and plastic tumblers also produce attractive shapes.

Commercial moulds can be bought at craft shops, these vary greatly in price from a few pence to a few pounds. They are usually made from rubber, rigid plastic, glass or metal and, of course, come in all manner of shapes and sizes. I would suggest, however, that before you buy any moulds, you look around the house. You'll be surprised at what you find, and it also helps to keep the cost down while you are making your first experiments.

Oil

Baby oil or olive oil is needed to *lightly* rub round the mould so that the candle can be removed without difficulty.

Wicking needle

A useful aid in threading the wick is a wicking needle, usually about 8" long and costing about 15 pence.

Double boiler

To melt wax it is necessary to do it over water, and not directly over dry heat. If you don't possess a double boiler, a heat resistant jug or bowl over an old saucepan will do. Melt the wax in the top container keeping the water away from the wax. In fact it's just like melting cooking chocolate!

Extras

You will also need some cotton wool, for wiping the mould with oil, masking tape, an old pair of tights, old newspapers and a heat resistant jug.

Process

Now that we've an idea of the various thing we use, let's talk about the making of a candle in its basic form.

Candle making can get a bit messy, so before anything else I usually change into old clothes and spread old newspapers over the floor. Let's face it, if wax should get spilt it will be a lot easier to clean up this way!

1 Fill the bottom half of your double boiler (or saucepan, if you are using this) with water and bring this to the boil.

2 Break up the wax into small pieces and, when the water has boiled, place these in the top half of the boiler (or bowl, if using a makeshift boiler). Reduce the heat so that the water is simmering. It is comparatively rare for wax to ignite, but just in case TURN OFF HEAT SUPPLY and COVER THE TOP OF THE PAN IMMEDIATELY. DO **NOT** USE WATER TO EXTINGUISH FIRE.

3 While the wax is heating slowly, prepare a mould for use. We shall use a length of drainpipe in this instance. With a tiny amount of oil, wipe out the inside of the pipe.

4 Cover one of the open ends of the pipe completely with masking tape.

5 Using a thick wick, tie one end of the wick to a pencil or piece of strong wire. Thread the other end of the wick through the wicking needle, and take it down the inside of the drainpipe mould and pull it through the taped end of the pipe. Secure the wick at the masking tape end with another small piece of tape, leaving about 2″ of spare wick. Make sure the pencil is resting across the middle of the pipe so the wick will be straight. The mould is now ready to use.

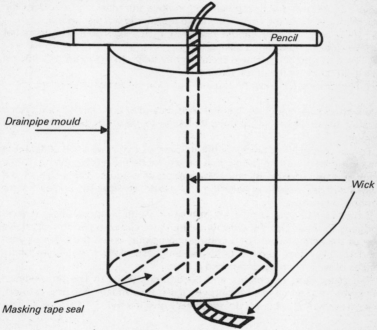

Pencil

Drainpipe mould

Wick

Masking tape seal

6 Back to the wax. When the wax has almost completely melted add to it (i) the dye (ii) 1 teaspoon of hardener (iii) perfume if necessary. (Half a dye disc and 1 teaspoon of hardener will do 2lb of wax) Keep wax, with all additives, on low heat and stir thoroughly with metal spoon until hardener granules have dissolved.

7 Test the temperature with your wax thermometer. I find 200°F is about right for most candles.

8 With a small heat resistant jug slowly transfer the wax from your melting container into the mould. Try to do this slowly and steadily to avoid air bubbles being trapped in the wax.

9 Fill mould to $\frac{1}{2}''$ below the top and leave to stand for a few moments. Then gently tap the side of the mould to release any trapped air.

10 When a thick skin has formed over the top of the candle (after about thirty minutes) pierce two or three holes down the length of the candle with your wicking needle and top up with more of the wax at 200°F. This process will need to be repeated two or three times. You will notice that as the candle sets a well forms in the top. This is due to the contraction of the wax as it cools. Top it up with liquid wax to make it level.

11 Leave candle in the mould in a cool place for several hours, preferably overnight, before removing.

12 Once the candle is set and cold, cut off the wick at the pencil end (now the bottom of your candle) and remove the masking tape from the top. With the aid of the oil on the mould the candle will just slide out.

13 If the bottom of the candle is uneven, melt it level on a very warm flat surface, for example an old baking tin.

14 To finish off the surface, polish lightly with old nylon tights, this will give a soft shine to the outer surface.

15 Trim the wick to $\frac{1}{2}''$ at the top and just look at the beautiful result.

The instructions I've given are for a basic candle, but candles don't need to stay plain. There are dozens of ways to vary candles with a little thought.

To use up the small amounts of left-over wax you will soon collect, set the wax in layers letting each stripe almost set before adding the next. The result will be a candle in any combination of colours. The angle of the stripes can be varied by securing the mould at different angles before pouring in the wax.

If the sides of your candle are broken or rough in appearance, a good dodge is to 'overdrip' the sides with liquid wax. Use a spoon and trickle wax of the same colour, or a contrasting colour, down the sides of your candle. The effect can be quite pleasing especially if you use toning shades of wax, such as orange and brown.

The sizes, shapes, colours and decorations you can use are endless. Once you've tried candle making you'll see how much simpler it is to do, than to read or talk about. I do hope you'll give it a try.

Useful addresses

1 Basic requirements can be bought at local craft shops. In Newcastle, where I often shop, 'Gemini', Shakespeare Street, Newcastle upon Tyne, are very useful.

2 There is also an excellent postal service from Candle Makers' Supplies, 28 Blythe Road, London W14 0HA.

3 Mrs J Darby, 64 Longridge Way, Cramlington, Northumberland. I will be glad to try to help you with any problems if you write enclosing an S.A.E.

Corn dollies
by Huelwen Fellows

People in ancient times found that some seed-bearing plants were good to eat, but they did not, as yet, know how to cultivate them, and so to ensure these plants would be there when needed, they created a goddess of fertility. Eventually these early people discovered that if they planted seeds in the fertile plains in the springtime, come autumn and they could reap a profitable harvest. So began farming, which at this time was mainly the task of the women, for the men were the hunters. These early farmers still believed that the spirit of the goddess of fertility lived in the fields, in the ears of the growing plants. Her spirit would die if all the crop was cut and threshed, so the best, or last sheaf of the harvest was fashioned into a corn idol, to ensure her spirit's safe keeping until sowing time next year. This protectress of the living, a wakener of new life was known by various names — the most widely known being goddess Ceres.

The corn idol was originally fashioned into the shape of a human being, to represent the goddess Ceres, and the making of the idol was an essential part of the fertility rites performed at the end of harvest. This form of corn dolly was known as the Corn Mother in Germany and the Mother Sheaf in Brittany, and in Britain it had many names as well, ranging from Kirk Maiden in Scotland to Ivy Girl in Kent.

No one really knows when or how the corn idol came to be made with the traditional spiral plait that we usually associate with the corn dolly. It is thought that the first plaited corn could have been the cornucopia, for symbolically it has been used in pagan worship to represent continuing plenty. Old documents suggest that we in Britain, at one time, offered goats' horns on altars set up to honour the sun god Apollo. It may be at this time, the time of the Roman occupation, that the first plaited corn dollies were introduced to our isles.

Wall drawings in the tomb of Tutankhamen show farming life at the time of the Pharaohs. The farmer is shown carrying home a plaited corn dolly. Thus we have a record of plaited corn dollies being made as early as 1343 BC.

The word corn is very general in meaning, covering the seed or plant of wheat, barley, oats, maize and rye. In fact cereal crops in general.

A corn dolly can be made in any shape or form, as long as it incorporates in it some grain-bearing ears of a growing crop. Corn dollies in Britain and Europe are traditionally made of wheat and look quite different from maize dolls made from the broad leaf of the sweet corn plant.

Barley is a popular crop, especially in northern parts of Britain, but the stem is too short and thin to use successfully for plaiting. Oat straw is probably the best in colour, being a really golden colour, but the stem tends to be too soft to hold its shape. Rye grows very tall and has a pale cream colour, although it is not a crop very widely grown. But wheat is grown in most parts of Britain, and is available to almost anyone who can visit the countryside at harvest time.

Modern methods of farming have necessitated the production of a wheat, short and solid in stem in order to withstand bad weather, and be standing for the combine harvester to complete its job. But there are a number of varieties of wheat that *can* be used. When choosing wheat for plaiting, certain properties are necessary to produce a good finished article: the stem, between the head and first joint, needs to be long, hollow and a good colour. Also, if possible, use straw grown without too much artificial fertilizer, for the latter tends to produce brittle straw. However, wheat is now grown especially for making corn dollies, of the long, hollow-stemmed, golden variety. Here are the names of some kinds of wheat that are suitable for making articles from corn: Elibe Lepeuple, Maris Widgeon, Maris Huntsman, Flamingo, Eclipse, Squarehead Master, Joss Cambier, Capelle.

There are certain traditional shapes used for corn dollies, which are quite often associated with particular parts of the country. These basic shapes are now often adapted to make more modern designs.

The traditional shapes include the horseshoe from Suffolk; the bell from Cambridgeshire; the cross, crown, anchor, and the crossed keys of St. Peter from Devonshire; the fan from the Border Counties and Wales, and the neck (a spiral with a loop on top), Mother Earth, rattle, cornucopia, favours and love knots found in all parts of Britain.

A typical adaptation of a traditional design to suit a modern need is the crossed keys of St. Peter being adapted to form a coming of age key.

Materials for making corn dollies

Strong thread — preferably linen
Medium weight florist's stub wire
Dried lavender
Dried flowers
Ribbon
Straw

Straw

Any hollow-stemmed corn, with a good length between head and first joint. For varieties see introduction to corn dollies. Some of these varieties are grown especially for corn dolly making, but try the wheat grown in your own area — it may be suitable. Please, do ask the farmer if you may cut a little from the edge of the field. The corn should be cut whilst the colour is just turning from green to gold, the heads are still upright, and the seed still secure in each head. This is usually about a week before the farmer combines his crop.

Cut the corn close to the ground. Just after it has been cut the corn is moist, and can be used immediately for plaiting. If you want to store it for future use, dry it thoroughly on racks in an airy place. Store in a mouse- and sparrow-free dry place, and the corn can be used up to a year or more later.

Equipment

Scissors
Wire cutters
Damp cloth (for keeping straw moist whilst working)
Large-eyed darning needle
Spring clothes peg
Tall jug (capable of taking boiling water)
Kettle

Preparing corn

1 Cut the corn above the first joint, and strip off the leaf or flag. Keep some of the corn with good heads for a special use, then cut the heads off the rest, the cut should be at an angle. Save some of the straw, below the first joint, to make the core of any padded corn article. This corn is used as a central filling around which you plait. Grade the cut straw by comparing the thickness over the bottom 8″. As a good guide compare with knitting needle sizes 8, 10 and 12 for thick, medium and fine straw.

2 The straw must be damp when used. Secure a bundle of graded straws with rubber bands, and place, thick end uppermost, in a tall receptacle. Pull one straw up from the bundle and hold this whilst pouring boiling water through the hollow straws. Roll straws in a damp cloth, and keep them covered in this whilst working. Use within 30 hours. After this, unused straws should be dried out. They can be redampened when required.

3 *Clove hitch.* This is used to tie several straws together. Make two loops as in Fig 1. Place loop 2 behind loop 1 as in Fig 2. Insert head end of straws through both loops.

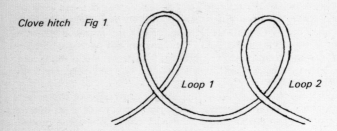

Clove hitch   Fig 1

Loop 1   *Loop 2*

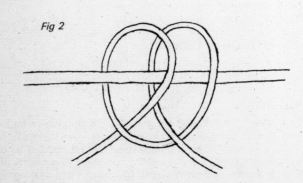

Fig 2

Five straw spiral plait

This is the basis of many corn dollies and is well worth practising.

1 Tie five straws tightly together with a clove hitch knot at the head ends.

2 Arrange straws out at points of the compass, with two straws to the east. Hold work in left hand, with the short ends of straw on top (see Fig 3).

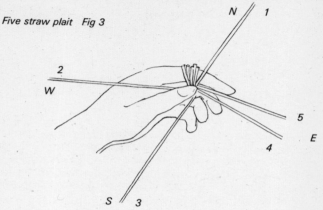

Five straw plait   Fig 3

3 Take straw 5 under straw 4 to the south, then over straw 4 to the north, laying it on top of straw 1 (see Fig 4). Hold these two straws together in the right hand. Let go of work with left hand and turn work clockwise.

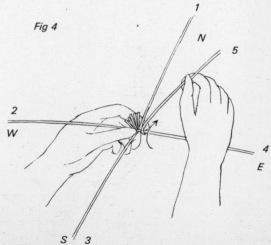

Fig 4

4 Replace work in left hand. Straws 1 and 5 are now in the east position (see Fig 5). Repeat stages 3 and 4 as work progresses.

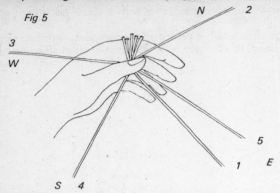

Fig 5

5 To keep work straight, the size of the working square must be kept constant, by laying the working straw so that it is level at the corner with the straw below. Plait round a pencil or dowel rod — the working straw will lay close to the core and the size of the square remain constant (see Fig 6). Looking at the inside of your plait you will see a square shape, but on the outside it makes a rounded spiral shape.

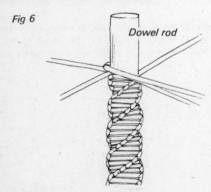

Fig 6

Dowel rod

6 Join in a new straw when:
  a) you come to the end of the straw
  b) the straw is discoloured
  c) the straw is hard

The straw is narrower at the head end than just above the first joint, which enables one to join two straws easily, by inserting the narrow end into the wider end. Cut off surplus straw close to the edge of the work at the corner, and insert a new straw for at least $\frac{1}{2}''$. The fold of the next working straw will cover the join.

7 To widen gradually, lay the working straw on top of, but slightly to the right-hand side of the straw pointing north. The shape of the corn dolly is varied by the degree to which one lays the working straw to the right of the north straw. To increase flat, that is to increase rapidly, lay the working straw side by side with, and to the right of, the north straw.

8 To narrow. The size of the working square is decreased by laying the working straw to the left of the straw pointing north, the space between the north straw and the working straw should be no more than the width of the straw.

NB It usually takes twice as many turns to decrease back to the original size than it took to increase.

Horseshoe — traditional corn dolly

1 Requires 25 medium straws and a 12″ stub wire.

2 Make a core of spare corn, using five 12″ straws with stub wire inserted through one straw. Secure with thread, or sparingly with clear adhesive tape.

3 Tie five of the medium straws tightly together with a clove hitch at the head ends. Plait a five straw spiral around prepared core. Plait to end of core.

4 With a large-eyed darning needle, thread ends of corn into end of plait and out again about 1″ from end (see Fig 7). Cut straw off close to work.

Fig 7

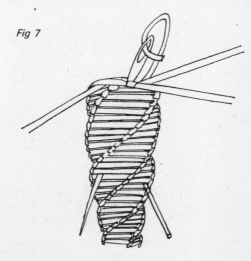

5 Bend horseshore whilst corn is still damp.

6 Decorate with corn heads and ribbon bow.

Blackberry basket — a traditional basket in spider's web plait with a five plait spiral border

1 You require 80 thick and 80 fine straws and six 18″ stub wires.

2 Take six long, thick straws and thread a stub wire through each. Tie the straws tightly together at the centre, keeping straws flat. Tie in one working straw also at the centre. Arrange wired straws out evenly to form spokes of a wheel.

3 Using the one working straw, take straw over two spokes and back under one, this forms the spider's web plait. Continue in this way, keeping spokes evenly spaced. Join in a new straw by cutting off old straw just beyond spoke. Insert new straw, taking it under the spoke and back over the join to continue sequence of over two spokes, under one. Continue until base measures 9″ in diameter.

4 Bend spokes up to make sides of basket and continue in spiders web plait until sides measure 3″ high.

5 Tie last straw to spoke and bend spokes across each space to the right. Tie off each one — A to B, B to C, etc (see Fig 8).

Blackberry basket   *Fig 8*

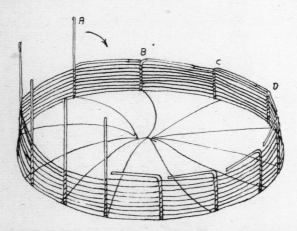

6 Make border. Make a five straw plait around one straw core without wire, to fit top of basket (approximately 30″ long). Thread in ends and tie ends together to make a circle. Sew neatly to top of basket.

Useful books

Corn Dollies by L. Sandford & P. Davis (Herefordshire Women's Institute 1958)

Decorative Straw Work by L. Sandford & P. Davis. 1964

Corn Dollies by L. Sandford (Herefordshire Women's Institute)

Corn Dollies by Margaret J. Knott (National Federation of Women's Institutes)

A Golden Dolly by M. & R. C. Lambeth

Straw Craft, More Golden Dollies by M. Lambeth

The Art of Weaving Corn Dollies by Stephen J. Reid

Useful addresses

Corn by the sheaf can be obtained from Armitage, West Hall Farm, Sedgeford, Hunstanton, Norfolk.

Prepared corn and corn dolly kits can be obtained from Felcraft, 15 Ludlow Avenue, North Shields, Tyne and Wear.

The Making of Wooden Toys
by Colin Sims

If we consider the word toy we have by definition 'a play-thing', 'a trinket or curiosity', 'not meant for real use'. Therefore the toy is not meant just for children and can play a very important part in all our lives. An example of this is the explosion onto the market, in the late 60's, of the 'executive toy', many based on scientific principles but toys none the less. From my own experience I know that some of the toys that I make are sitting very proudly on office desks. Some are even collected and locked away 'so that the kids can't play with them and spoil them'. But in general we equate toys with children. Ask an adult why they have a toy and it is excused as a puzzle, game, a demonstration of scientific principle, a thing of beauty in its own right, anything rather than admit to the need for a play-thing.

My feeling is that if you, as an adult, want an expensive toy, a train set etc, then admit it, buy it for yourself, don't use little Jimmy as an excuse. There must be millions of pounds worth of toys mouldering away in attics and cupboards across the country, and why, because they were bought too soon, they were too sophisticated. So we have arrived at an important factor — *Simplicity*.

We hear a lot these days of educational toys. I prefer not to talk of toys in the context of education. In the broadest sense of the word all toys may be considered educational, but in the strictest sense an educational toy is a device to assist or enhance methods of teaching. A toy can and should in a lot of cases be inspirational, which to my mind brings us once again to *simplicity*, but this time allied to purpose, in other words, the look and feel of the thing in use. Although to say this is a generalisation, a well-designed artefact usually functions well.

If we look at the child as a baby, its first toys are soft and cuddly, or hand objects which make a noise, usually plastic rattles and rings which are hung out of reach on prams and cots (these could quite easily be made of wood). At this stage the child is developing all its senses and because of the predominance of soft toys is somewhat limited in experience. But because of physical contact with its immediate surroundings, cot, pram, even mother, the child develops an awareness of hard as well as soft surfaces. So an early toy (object) could well be a small piece of hardwood, shaped and smoothed into the form of a bone or dumb-bell with the centre (barrel) of a diameter which would allow the hand to grip it, and the ends large enough to give the sense of smoothness and hardness.

The next stage is when the child is sitting up and the obvious choice here are some blocks and strips of wood for moving around and piling up. Again, these are best made in hardwood although softwood with a polyurethane finish is just as suitable. They should be of a size which will allow the child to pick them up, but not of a regular shape (square, rounded, triangluar, flat and long) thereby enabling the child to identify edges, corners, holes and surfaces. You could also make some slightly larger pieces with simple wooden, well secured wheels, do not try and make them look like anything in particular. At this stage the child will only appreciate the moving action.

Beyond this stage it would be as well to stop and consider individual hand-made toys. Certain factors will affect your decisions about whether you will continue making them as your child grows, because we are about to move into an area where you will need more than just a saw and sandpaper. The most basic toy for the growing child will require a tool kit that will grow along with your skill. Basic requirements would be covered by acquiring the tools listed below.

Tools and materials

Portable vice
Small tenon saw
Coping saw
Small hammer and fine nail punch
Screwdriver
Square
Pullout steel rule or 2ft wooden rule
Flat file with plain edges
Retractable knife with replaceable blades
Electric drill and bits
Cork sandpaper block

The tool kit is, of course, only one of the starting points, another is materials. When buying materials, probably from your local handicraft or Do-It-Yourself supplier, there are a few things to consider.

Planed timber comes in varying lengths, widths and thicknesses. The length is usually gauged in multiples of a foot (or standard metric lengths). Remember that a bought piece of wood, width 2'', thickness 1'' will measure marginally less as a finished item so take this into consideration if making joints etc.

Sheet materials, plywood, blockboard, handboard, chipboard in varying thicknesses, all come in manufactured 8' x 4' sheets or are cut down to smaller standard sheets, 4' x 4', 2' x 2' etc. If you want sheets cut to non-standard sizes there will probably be a cutting charge. Contrary to popular opinion, it is not always cheaper to use 'offcuts', as they are not always readily available (unless you are fortunate enough to have a firm locally that deals in factory offcuts) and the result may be that you will have to compromise on your design.

Your local supplier is in business to encourage peole to make things themselves and is consequently usually prepared to help by answering all but the silliest questions. However, he is not there to do your design work for you, so go knowing what you want. Knowing what you want has some basic rules and facts, some of which have already been mentioned, but perhaps we should make another list of considerations.

1 Keep the design simple
2 Understand the purpose of the toy
3 Know the limitations of yourself, as a carpenter, and of the materials
4 Safety in use

All these rules bear one upon the other and boil down to giving considerable thought to what you are going to make before you buy materials. Have a look around at what is available, it is no good making a wheeled toy if after you have started you find you cannot purchase wheels of the kind you want. Stick to standard size timber. Work within the limitations of your tool kit or you may find yourself having to buy an expensive tool for which you might not have much use in the future.

Safety

Safety obviously needs thinking about and this mainly concerns tools. Cheap tools are not so cheap in the long run. Buy good quality pieces and look after them. There is nothing so dangerous to the wood-worker as blunt and wobbly tools. A blunt saw can slip and take a lot of skin, or worse, with it, and the head coming off a hammer in mid-stroke is lethal.

The main hazard to safety with constructed toys as opposed to solid toys is bad joints. It is worth practising cutting joints, again the sharp saw is necessary, especially butt joints which are pinned and glued.

Nails and pins on larger toys are not particularly dangerous as long as they are used in conjunction with the well-cut joint and good quality woodworking adhesive (not impact adhesive which is for sticking things on large flat surfaces) and this joint will be far stronger than the timber it is holding together. Always punch down the nail heads and fill holes with a proprietary stopper.

The ultimate safe, strong joint is that which is glued and dowelled. But this is a fairly sophisticated technique which requires very accurate marking out and drilling (or the purchase of a dowel jig which is fairly expensive for occasional use). A dowel jig may be made out of scrap hardwood but this, in itself, requies accurate drilling which means having the use of a vertical drill press. There are commercially manufactured jointing pieces available which can be useful for box construction. They consist of two plastic blocks which are screwed one to each side of the corner and are then drawn together by screwing a bolt through both blocks. This method, although not so neat as the traditional ones, does have the one advantage that it is possible to dismantle the box if necessary.

Another thing that has a bearing on safety as well as the practicability of the toy is the finish. Any wood, even hardwood, splinters. Therefore, always try for a smooth, even streamlined finish. If you use screws, countersink them and fill over as with the nails. If this is not practical, use a screw cup under the head or use round head screws. Watch out for any